to Unc
from
Amanda
& Edee

Puff away!

Christmas 1997

THE

HANDBOOK

THE

HANDBOOK

A BUYER'S GUIDE
TO THE WORLD'S FINEST CIGAR BRANDS

MARK STÜCKLIN

A QUINTET BOOK

This edition published by
Barnes & Noble, Inc.,
by arrangement with Quintet Books Ltd
1997 Barnes & Noble Books

ISBN 0-7607-0434-1

M 10 9 8 7 6 5 4 3 2

This book was designed and produced by
Quintet Publishing Limited
6 Blundell Street
London N7 9BH

Creative Director: Richard Dewing
Art Director: Silke Braun
Designer: Ian Hunt
Senior Editor: Anna Briffa
Photographer: Keith Waterton

Typeset in Great Britain by
Central Southern Typesetters, Eastbourne
Manufactured in Singapore by
Eray Scan Pte Ltd
Printed in China by
Leefung-Asco Printers Ltd

CONTENTS

FOREWORD

I couldn't have been a lad of more than eight years on that day my father steered up our drive in his new XJ6 Jaguar saloon, with its midnight blue lacquer and deep navy blue interior. The late afternoon sun sent a cascade of glimmering rays off its concupiscent bonnet, and for an instant the XJ6 seemed a sailfish, taut against the line, skirting the watery surface of our steep driveway. With all the curiosity that eight years bestows on a child, I hurried to the passenger door and climbed in to greet my father. I will never forget the intoxicating mélange of aromas I encountered as I clambered onto the seat: the leather cushions, the walnut trim, the wool carpet—and a Montecristo No. 2. It wasn't as if I'd never smelled a cigar before, but that day was different, magical. Just like that sailfish, I was hooked!

The far-distant memories of how or why we ventured out to smoke our first cigars—almost all of us recall with some nostalgia, in the way one might remember a past lover from youthful days. But unlike such youthful lovers, cigars continue to evoke passion and pleasure in a way that nothing else quite does. Each cigar is a new and sensual experience which instantly distinguishes the smoker from those around him. When two cigar enthusiasts meet, a bond is created that words can do little to convey. Cigars embody a certain sense of fraternity which spans generations, diminishes political differences, and somehow makes all quarreling suddenly seem petty.

I founded *Smoke* magazine with the idea that each issue should be as precious and unique as smoking a fine cigar. *The Cigar Handbook* takes the same approach. Each brand is dealt with individually. They are not compared to each other for either positive or negative criticism, but stand as a single experience in their own right. This book carries a great deal of information for its size, so pick out a quiet place, light a fine cigar, and read on!

Aaron Sigmond
New York City
January 1997

AARON SIGMOND *is the creator and founding editor-in-chief of* Smoke *magazine. Since its inception in 1995, Smoke has been one of the fastest growing magazines in publishing history and is now enjoyed by cigar devotees in countries around the world.*

INTRODUCTION

The cigar boom of the past few years has encouraged an explosion of new brands on retailer's shelves alongside the established names. Together they present a bewildering selection to choose from. This book has been written to serve as a guide to any adventurous smoker wishing to explore.

Albeit briefly, it also endeavors in Part I to shed some light on how cigars are made, on what makes them taste the way they do, and on how best to go about enjoying them. In my experience the more I have learnt about the huge effort and skill that goes into making great cigars the more I have appreciated them.

Whether you have been smoking cigars for many years or have only recently discovered their delights, I hope you find information in the following pages that furthers your pleasure.

I would like to thank Simon Chase, Benjamin Menendez, Edward Butler, and my Editor Anna Briffa for helping me to write this handbook.

Mark Stücklin
London, 1997

PART I

Introduction to Premium Cigars

WHAT IS A PREMIUM CIGAR?

The vast majority of cigars are machine-made short-filler cigars and differ greatly in manufacturing processes, structure, quality, and price from premium cigars. They earn the title of "cigar" because they are made with a tobacco filler, binder, and wrapper.

A premium cigar is one that is made entirely by hand using whole and intact tobacco leaves for filler. These long filler leaves are arranged and secured in a binder leaf by hand to make a "bunch" (in Cuba bunching is always done exclusively by hand, but in other countries bunching is typically done with the help of a simple hand-operated bunching device). A wrapper leaf is then rolled around the bunch, also by hand.

It takes considerable time and skill to make each premium cigar, and manufacturers reserve the very best tobacco for them. The precision of the handmaking process, the structure of the resulting cigar, and the quality of leaf used mean that premium cigars are the best available and stand in a class of their own.

Because of the absence of strict industry-wide rules governing the use of the term "handmade" dubious claims have inevitably been made that exploit the appeal of the term with little justification. Especially in the North American market there are cigars made almost entirely by machine which are then sold as "handmade" on the strength of a small patch of tobacco applied by hand to the head of the cigar. This can be considered as grossly misleading to the consumer.

Far less misleading are cigars sold as "handmade" that have been machine-bunched using long filler leaves which are then dressed in a wrapper by hand. Many of the best-selling premium brands include a number of cigars made in this way. Nevertheless a truly premium cigar is one made *entirely* by hand, and it is on these cigars that this guide will focus.

SURROUNDED BY THE TOOLS OF HER TRADE, A CUBAN CIGAR ROLLER FINISHES OFF A HANDROLLED CIGAR.

FILLERS, BINDERS, AND WRAPPERS

FILLER

The filler is the inside of a cigar, where most of the blending takes place. Filler leaves, chosen for flavor, aroma, and burning qualities, are mixed together in proportions that combine to produce a desired style.

Filler tobacco is cultivated in several different countries around the world from seed strains suited to producing flavorful leaves. Grown in direct sunlight which encourages intensity of flavor, the leaves are harvested in stages starting at the bottom of the bush and moving upwards.

From the base of the plant come leaves thin in texture and light in flavor, known as *volado* in Cuba and other Spanish speaking countries. Once harvested these leaves are dried in a 45-day long process known as air curing. In curing, the leaves change from green to brown as chlorophyll turns to carotene. After curing the leaves go to fermentation, a natural chemical process rather like composting in which the aggressive elements of the leaf such as acidity, tar, and nicotine are reduced. It is easy to either under-do or over-cook leaf in fermentation, both of which ruin it, so fermentations are carefully managed according to the ability of the leaf to stand up to the process. Because of *volado's* delicacy it can only handle two gentle fermentations, after which it is baled and left to rest before being used to make cigars. In the blend *volado* is used on the one hand as a neutral filler to dilute the strength of other richer leaves, and on the other to help the cigar to burn evenly because of its excellent combustible qualities.

From the center of the plant come leaves of medium body and texture known as *seco*, which go through the same curing process as *volado*, but need more vigorous fermentations followed by a longer ageing period in bale. *Seco* leaves are typically the backbone of a cigar's blend due to their all-round flavor and burning properties.

From the crown of the plant come thick, full-bodied leaves known as *ligero* which play bass in the cigar's band of flavors. After curing, *ligero* needs several intense fermentations and then up to two years or more resting in bale before blending. *Ligero* has to be used cautiously in blends in order to avoid creating overpowering cigars.

BINDER

The binder leaf goes around the blend of filler leaves and secures them in what is known as the bunch. Leaf intended to be used as binder has its entire central vein removed thus leaving the leaf in two halves. In Cuba they tend to lay one half on top of the other and then use both halves as a two-ply binder for one bunch, whereas in other countries they typically use just one half-leaf binder per bunch. Binder leaves are taken from the same plants as filler leaves and go through the same curing, fermentation, and ageing processes.

Binder leaves need to burn well and be big enough to perform the job of securing the filler leaves from head to foot. For these reasons binder leaves are taken either from the *volado*, or from the very lowest sections of the *seco* pickings.

CUBAN CIGAR ROLLERS, KNOWN AS *TORCEDORS*, AT WORK.

CIGAR TOBACCO PRODUCTION

TOBACCO CROPS GROWING IN CUBA.

PINAR DEL RIO PROVINCE, CUBA. HARVESTED FILLER LEAVES ARE HUNG IN PAIRS OVER POLES CALLED *CUJES*, WHICH ARE THEN RACKED IN CURING BARNS.

TOBACCO LEAVES IN THE EARLY STAGES OF AIR CURING.

A TOBACCO PLANTATION IN BRAZIL.

FILLER LEAVES BEING HARVESTED.

A *CASA DE TABACO* OR CURING BARN. THESE ARE BUILT ON THE PLANTATIONS.

WRAPPER

A wrapper leaf dresses the bunch and gives a cigar its public face. It needs to be large enough, silky in texture, and free of any damage or blemishes in order to make the cigar look attractive.

The seed strains used to grow filler leaves do not produce satisfactory wrappers so different strains have been developed. Once again several seed strains are used to grow wrappers in different parts of the world, two famous examples being the Connecticut Shade strain from Connecticut, U.S.A., and the Corojo strain from Cuba.

STRETCHING A WRAPPER LEAF AROUND A BUNCH.

TRIMMING A WRAPPER LEAF TO SIZE WITH A "CHAVETA" OR CIGAR ROLLER'S BLADE.

Most premium cigar wrappers are grown under tents of muslin that shelter the leaves from direct sunlight. This method, called shade growing or *tapado* (covered), encourages the leaves to grow large and silky and protects them to a certain extent from damage.

Perfect wrappers are extremely difficult to grow as the slightest damage or stain incurred at any stage can render them useless as wrappers. This makes them the rarest and most expensive part of any cigar and can sometimes severely constrain cigar production.

Wrapper leaves are also harvested in stages starting with the bottom of the plant, but normally only leaves from the middle two thirds of the plant go on to qualify as wrappers since only these leaves are of the right size and texture. Once harvested the leaves are then cured, fermented, and aged in a similar way to filler leaves, but undergo a far more exacting grading and selection process. They also have their entire central vein removed, leaving them in two halves, before arriving at the roller's bench.

Wrapper colors

Surprisingly perhaps, color grading is one of the most complex parts of cigar production, with handmade cigars coming in a great variety of colors and shades, ranging from black, through brown, to light green. Color classifications tend to differ from country to country, and manufacturer to manufacturer, making sweeping and watertight claims about color difficult. This notwithstanding, in the chart below are listed the seven basic categories of colors as far as it is possible to group them.

It should be noted that wrappers from the two opposite ends of the color spectrum typically undergo treatments that differ in some important aspects to the one detailed above.

Cigars with black or very dark wrappers are called *oscuro*, which means dark in Spanish, or *maduro*, which means ripe. Normally these are thick textured wrappers which are sun grown, not shade grown, and undergo a boiling process known as "cooking" which gives them their dark color and strong taste.

Cigars with light green wrappers are variously described as *double claro*, AMS (American Market Selection) or *candela*. To produce these, heaters are used to accelerate the curing process of shade grown wrappers in such a way that prevents all of the chlorophyll turning into carotene and fixes the green color. Once very popular in the American market, these wrappers are only remarkable for their color and have few admirers today.

The great majority of wrappers presently produced fall somewhere between pale brown (*claro*) and dark brown (*colorado maduro*) as these wrappers consistently offer the most popular aroma, flavor, and appearance.

WRAPPER COLORS.
FROM LEFT TO RIGHT: 1) DOUBLE CLARO/AMS/CANDELA: 2) CLARO: 3) COLORADO CLARO: 4) COLORADO: 5) COLORADO MADURO: 6) MADURO: 7) OSCURO.

THE ADVANTAGES OF HANDMADE LONG-FILLER CIGARS

Handmade long-filler cigars are the best in the world, and not simply because the finest tobacco is reserved for making them. Every aspect of their structure is designed to increase the pleasure of smoking through harmony of flavor, ease of draw, and coolness of smoke.

THE ASSEMBLY PROCESS

The term "long filler" means that the *volado*, *seco*, and *ligero* filler leaves are used intact, apart from the thickest third of the central vein which is removed in a process known as frog-stripping. This stands in contrast to "short filler", used in most machine-made cigars, where the filler leaves have been broken down into many little pieces.

In the cigar factory the buncher will pick exact proportions of each type of filler leaf, in keeping with the blend's specifications, and carefully position them by hand before securing them with a binder. The bunch is then pressed in a mold for a minimum of half an hour to give it rigidity, before a wrapper leaf is skilfully rolled around it by hand.

EFFECTS ON SMOKING EXPERIENCE

Arranging long filler by hand means that blends can be carefully and precisely constructed so that, when the cigar is smoked, its flavors develop in a harmonious way.

The filler leaves are laid in the bunch with their tips at the foot end (the end you light) and their stem ends at the head (the end you draw from). The lightest part of the leaf is the tip, while the richest part is the stem end. Therefore as you smoke down the cigar you travel through flavor zones in the leaf of increasing richness. A consistent development of flavor is thus achieved as flavor zones are encountered in a progressive order, rather than in the chaotic fashion that is typical of short filler.

Furthermore the leaves are placed so that the *ligero*, the thickest and the slowest burner, is in the middle of the cigar surrounded by *seco* and *volado*, which are much better burners. The result is a cigar that burns down evenly rather than lopsidedly.

The way the filler leaves have been folded and concertina'd results in natural passages in the folds of the leaves for the smoke to travel down without hindrance. Also the axis the leaves are on, which is always in a head to foot direction, means that you smoke with the grain of the leaf rather than against it. This should contribute to a good draw and even burn, and can support a long ash which in itself testifies to the quality of the cigar's construction.

LOOKING DOWN THE FOOT OF A CIGAR. THE HEAVIER LEAVES SHOULD BE FOUND IN THE CENTER.

CIGAR TOBACCO BY COUNTRY OF ORIGIN

Handmade cigars are produced in several countries including Cuba, Jamaica, the Dominican Republic, Honduras, Nicaragua, Brazil, Mexico, the Philippines, and the United States among others.

If cigars can be recognized by certain characteristics as being typical of one or other country, permitting talk of a Honduran style or a Dominican style, then as a cigar smoker it helps to be able to identify national styles, and establish preferences between them.

The Havana style is the easiest to spot because Habanos are always made from one hundred percent locally grown tobacco that is distinctive in character. But trying to identify styles typical of other countries is difficult as many of their manufacturers blend premium tobacco from all over the world into their cigars. Therefore it is only possible to clearly identify national styles to the extent that manufacturers use tobacco grown locally.

Nevertheless, here is a very brief look at some of the main cigar-producing countries and the styles of tobaccos they host.

CUBA

Cuba has the longest tradition of cigar making going back to 1492 and beyond. To Cuba, more than anywhere, we owe the development over the last two centuries of the long-filler handmade cigar. The resulting depth of experience and understanding that permeates every level of the Cuban cigar industry supports the creation of truly great cigars.

Also to be found in Cuba is a confluence of soil and climate that permits the production of some of the best cigar tobacco in the world. In the Vuelta Abajo and Partido regions, both to the west of Havana, there are ideal conditions for growing outstanding cigar tobacco. All handmade Havana cigars are produced with tobacco grown exclusively in these two regions. It is unsurprising therefore that, although all the Havana brands are delightfully individual, there emerges an unmistakable Havana style that they all reflect to some degree.

A CUBAN *VEGUERO* (TOBACCO GROWER) AT WORK.

A TYPICAL SCENE ON A TOBACCO PLANTATION IN THE PINAR DEL RIO PROVINCE OF CUBA.

"New World"

Christopher Columbus discovered Cuba along with the rest of the New World in 1492, so strictly speaking it is nonsense to talk of the "New World" in contrast to Cuba. However in the wine industry the term "New World" describes countries recently established as producers of excellent wine; similarly in a cigar context the term is not used literally, but rather in a way that distinguishes between the traditional producer—Cuba—and the other countries emerging as producers of cigars of impressive quality.

The Dominican Republic

From the "New World" group the Dominican Republic hosts many of the most capable manufacturers in the industry today. The Dominican Republic also grows excellent filler and binder leaf from two seed strains known as Olor and Piloto Cubano in the fertile Cibao valley in the north west of the country. Most Dominican cigar factories use this locally grown leaf in their blends, although usually it is blended with imported leaf. Dominican tobacco is characteristically mellow and sweet.

Honduras and Nicaragua

After understandable and massive setbacks due to the sad troubles that plagued Central America in the 1970s and 1980s, both Honduras and Nicaragua are in the process of re-establishing their reputations as premium-cigar producing countries. Tobacco cultivation is once again in full swing and cigar factories are being established and expanded in both countries to work with the locally grown leaf. The two countries cultivate a very similar style of tobacco which at its best is full-bodied and spicy.

Jamaica

During the Second World War and for the two decades that followed, Jamaica was, after Cuba and the United States, one of the biggest producers of premium cigars. After this golden age, and somewhat mirroring the overall premium cigar market, the Jamaican cigar industry went into gradual decline, bottoming out in the early 1990s when no cigar tobacco was being cultivated and only one premium cigar factory was still running—that of Cifuentes y Cia, where Macanudo and Temple Hall are produced. However, to the delight of the Jamaican Government this situation is changing as the Jamaica Tobacco Co. (owned by Consolidated and producing Royal Jamaica) returns to a new plant

Tending to young plants in Mexico.

and Old England Farms Ltd. once again begins to cultivate filler tobacco on Jamaican soil. This is a welcome development for smokers of premiums as Jamaica is quite capable of producing high-quality filler leaves and excellent cigars if leaf growers and cigar men of a high enough caliber invest their time and money in the country.

Tobacco grown locally in Jamaica is light in flavor, and many producers consider it too light to be used on its own. However, when used in tandem with richer tobaccos from other countries, it is capable of bringing harmony and balance to a blend.

Mexico

Mexico grows tobacco that cigar producers consider to be relatively strong and sweet. Many producers outside of Cuba use some Mexican tobacco in their blends to introduce these characteristics to their cigars, but until recently in Mexican cigar factories, only locally grown leaf was used—a situation that was encouraged by Mexican law. However, since a partial deregulation of the local cigar industry, manufacturers based there are beginning to blend tobacco from other countries into their cigars.

The United States of America

The United States has a long tradition of premium cigar making that has always been symbiotically related to events in Cuba. When the U.S. first imposed tariffs on imported cigars in the middle of the 19th century, U.S. cigar companies responded by importing Cuban tobacco and then manufacturing cigars in factories in Key West and Tampa. Many Cuban cigar rollers emigrated to the U.S. to work in these factories, and so it was that the "Clear Havana" was born—cigars rolled in the United States exclusively out of Cuban tobacco. Clear Havanas are no longer made in the U.S. since the trade embargo prohibits the use of Cuban tobacco, but the presence of many highly skilled Cuban cigar-rollers who emigrated to Florida after the revolution of 1959 supports the production of premium cigars in the United States.

The only cigar tobacco grown in the United States is Connecticut Shade which, as the name suggests, is shade-grown wrapper from the Connecticut river valley. Fantastic in texture and appearance this is the most popular wrapper leaf with "New World" manufacturers of premium cigars. Most Connecticut Shade wrapper leaves have a slightly yellowish hue to them, and are generally characterized by a dry taste.

Tobacco workers harvesting in Mexico.

FLAVORS

The following factors determine how a cigar will smoke and what it will taste like:

- The blend
- The cigar's condition at time of smoking
- The age of a cigar
- The state of the smoker's palate

THE BLEND

The soil in which the tobacco is grown, the unique weather conditions of each growing season, and the skill of the leaf men who decide on the fermentation and ageing of each bale after harvest all combine to shape the character of the leaf that arrives in the blending department.

The *ligero*, *seco*, and *volado* filler leaves will all be different in character, as will the binder and the wrapper. The blender has to understand how each of these will harmonize with the others to achieve the desired result—a good burning cigar whose flavor is in keeping with the brand's style; only then can he or she decide on the exact proportions of *ligero*, *seco*, and *volado* to go into the blend.

Simplifying the equation, the more *ligero* and less *volado* there is in the filler blend, the richer the cigar will be, and conversely the more *volado* and less *ligero*, the lighter it will be.

The wrapper's influence on flavor is a matter of some debate. Cuban producers claim that wrappers have little influence on the taste of a cigar, while many "New World" manufacturers believe that wrappers provide fifty percent or more of the overall flavor. What is beyond contention is that wrappers have a powerful visual impact and often shape the smoker's subjective expectations prior to lighting, leading them to believe for example that a dark oily wrapper heralds a rich, full-flavored smoke. Such expectations should be put to one side, and each cigar smoked with an open mind regardless of wrapper color; it is after all, only a very small part of the cigar.

Having said this, however, I believe that wrappers do contribute *something* to the flavor of a cigar, with dark wrappers supplying sweetness and light wrappers dryness.

CONDITION

In the same way that temperature influences the ability of wine to fully open up and express its flavor, the moisture content of a cigar is active in determining how well a cigar will smoke and whether it will realize its flavor potential.

Cigars smoked when they are too wet do not burn well, and require constant re-lighting. The excessive moisture makes them taste sharp or aggressive. On the other hand over-dry cigars burn too hot and readily, and have a dry, closed quality about them that has variously been described as dusty and acrid.

Only a cigar in perfect condition at the time of smoking really has any chance of tasting great. A simple and reliable way to test the condition of a cigar is to hold it between your thumb and index finger and squeeze gently. If it feels firm but springy then it is in good condition; hard and brittle means too dry, soft and spongy means too wet.

How to go about keeping cigars in good condition, and what to do about those that have fallen out of condition will be dealt with on pages 22–24.

AGE

Once a cigar has been rolled the active elements present in the tobacco leaf begin to react together in such a way that, if the cigar is kept in correct conditions that allow it to remain "alive," the character of the cigar changes over time. It is a very slow and gradual process, but over the course of years a cigar's flavors develop, becoming softer and rounder with time.

Immediately after rolling all cigars are aged for a minimum of 30 days in a cedar-lined room known as the *escaparate*. During this time the cigars rest after the rigors of rolling, shedding moisture and amonia, and arrive in tolerable smoking condition after approximately one month. The cigars are then sorted, boxed, and shipped, and any amount of time, from a couple of months to a number of years, can elapse between the cigars completing the minimum 30 days ageing and appearing for sale on a retailer's shelves.

Once upon a time, especially in the United Kingdom, shippers and retailers used to age cigars for many years before offering them for sale to customers. However the situation of the moment is such that as soon as cigars are produced they are shipped and sold in almost no time, which means there are few cigars of impressive maturity appearing on retailers shelves. Cigars of five, ten, fifteen, or more years are very difficult to acquire now, and therefore rare is the pleasure of smoking well aged cigars with all their finesse and smooth harmony of flavors. Young cigars have all the flavor of older ones but they just don't have quite the same polish.

Not all cigars benefit from lengthy ageing as, to go the distance, a cigar has to have a sufficient amount of guts in the first place. Therefore mild cigars with little body have to be smoked young as their flavors will fade away to nothing in a few short years. Cigars with rich blends and leaves brimming with natural oils benefit the most from long-term ageing.

THE STATE OF THE SMOKER'S PALATE

As Plato once demonstrated, the same wine can taste bitter or sweet depending on the state of mind and health of the person doing the drinking. Poor Plato never had the opportunity to philosophize in the company of a fine cigar, but the point he made is as relevant to cigars as it is to wine; the flavors of a great cigar will be missed or seem dull if the cigar is smoked at the wrong time.

The number of cigars you smoke in a day and the order in which you smoke them affect the ability of your palate to detect flavors. For a start too many cigars smoked in a day will leave the palate tasting like an old boot-polish rag. This dulls the palate and leads to diminishing returns on each cigar smoked once the palate has had enough. "Enough" differs according to the individual, so you have to discover your own limit and then aim to keep below it.

THE RIGHT CIGAR FOR THE MOMENT

To best appreciate a cigar's flavors the smoker's sensory equipment charged with the job of capturing and savoring the flavor must be in the best shape for doing this effectively. This means that light cigars should be avoided after very rich food as the palate will not be best disposed to detecting faint flavors, and rich cigars are not the ideal epilog to light food, as the loud flavors come as a shock to the palate tuned to gentle flavors. Rich cigars best compliment rich food and drink, and vise versa.

If you wish to smoke more than one cigar in a day then it is sensible to smoke cigars of progressively fuller flavor. The logic behind this is if you smoke a light cigar after a full-flavored one, you will not be able to appreciate the qualities of the second cigar, so for full enjoyment the next cigar you smoke should be as rich or richer than the one you have just finished. It follows from this that you need to buy a couple of different cigar brands that offer you this progression of flavor needed to furnish a good day's smoking.

SHAPES AND SIZES

All cigars are described by length, quoted in inches, and by girth—known as the ring gauge—which is quoted in 64ths of an inch.

Manufacturers give retail names like "Corona" and "Churchill" to the sizes they produce, and somewhat unhelpfully they often chose the same name to describe different sizes, resulting in no exact harmony between common names and the sizes they denote. However the common names do usually correspond to an approximate size, so you can be confident that a cigar called Churchill will be a substantial one, whatever its exact dimensions.

The vast majority of premium brands come in a number of handmade sizes (*vitolas*), with the Cuban Punch marque holding the present record of 34 different handmade *vitolas*. Many established brands offer between ten and twenty *vitolas*, and in order to choose the right size for a particular occasion one needs to understand what part size plays in determining the character of a cigar.

An obvious size-related consideration is how much time you have during which to smoke. A Montecristo "A" (9¼" x 47) demands three or more hours of attention and so should only be chosen when time is abundant. On the other hand the Demi-Tasse from Bolivar, which as its factory name (*Entreacto*) suggests was originally designed for smoking during the interval at the theater, takes a mere 15 minutes to smoke. The best counsel is to choose a size that will allow you to relax given the time available.

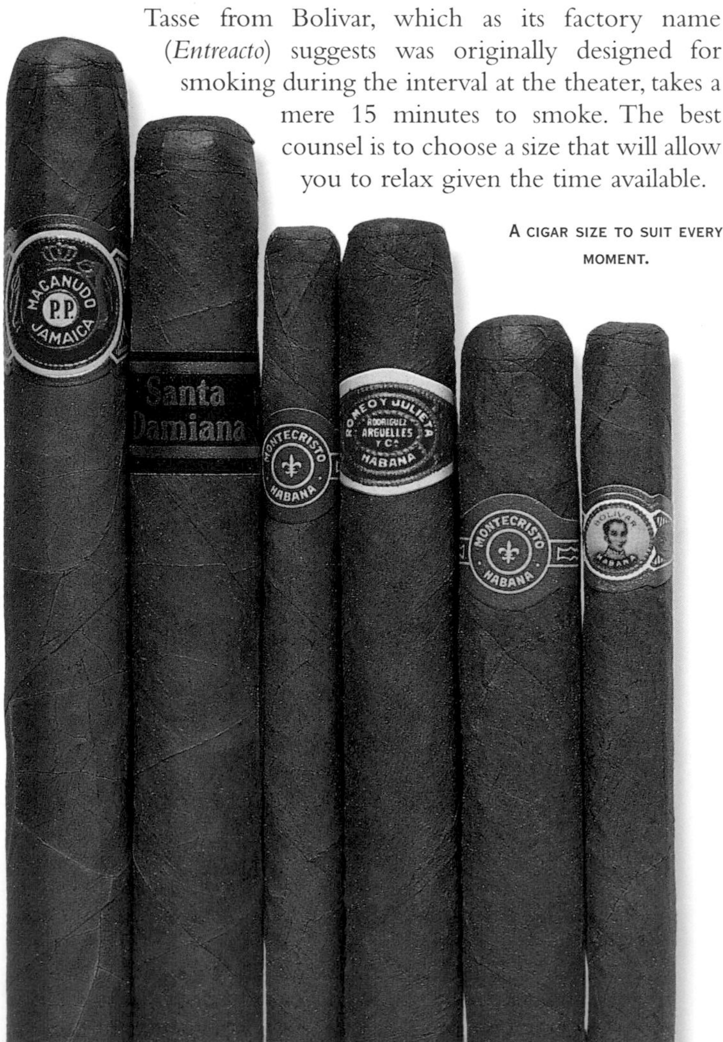

A CIGAR SIZE TO SUIT EVERY MOMENT.

THE EFFECT OF LENGTH AND GIRTH ON CHARACTER

The longer a cigar is the milder and cooler it will be when you first light it. The further down the cigar you smoke the richer and warmer it becomes, which means long cigars develop more in the course of being smoked than short ones do. Although not as rich in ability to develop during smoking, shorter cigars are appreciated for revealing their true character straight away, and offering a concentrated blast of flavor that does not demand too much of your time.

The fatter a cigar is, the more potential for complexity and fullness of flavor it has as it is girth that determines how many leaves or "ingredients" can be used in constructing the filler blend. Rather like cooking, the greater the number of ingredients used, the greater will be the end mix of flavors, assuming the blending and proportions are right. So a heavy girth should be chosen when rich and complex flavors are sought.

Slender gauge cigars tend to produce light and delicate flavors as the thin girth often prevents the use of any *ligero* in the blend. Furthermore narrow gauges prohibit the smoker from drawing off any great volume of smoke which limits the impact of flavor.

Standard ring gauge cigars are the most popular for good reason; chubby enough to deliver flavor and complexity, they are not so girthy as to be overwhelming, and burn at a slow and steady pace if well constructed.

DIFFERENT SHAPES

The great majority of premium cigars available today are *parejo* or straight-sided cigars. However for a couple of decades before and after the turn of the last century *figurado* or shaped cigars were the norm. By the late 1930s the *figurado* format was out of fashion and the switch to the *parejo* was almost complete, and since then practically the only *figurado* to survive this neglect has been the pyramid shape most famously embodied by the Montecristo No.2. However we are witnessing fashion turning full circle as *figurados* become more popular, a shift clearly affirmed by the launch of Cuaba, a Cuban brand exclusively comprised of different-sized figurados (see page 37).

PAREJOS (STRAIGHT SIDED) AND *SEMI-FIGURADOS* (PYRAMID SHAPED).

HUMIDIFICATION

As the ideal conditions for keeping cigars are not naturally found in most of our homes we have to place our cigars in humidors. Humidors are designed to ensure that cigars are stored in the correct conditions. Humidors of varying degrees of sophistication are available, ranging from a simple box equipped with a humidification unit to a complex fully-automated container linked by satellite to a central global control center.

A DESK-TOP HUMIDOR. ON THE INSIDE LID IS A HUMIDIFER AND A HYGROMETER FOR MEASURING THE HUMIDITY LEVEL.

The ideal conditions in which to keep cigars are sixty-five to seventy percent Relative Humidity (RH) and 61°–64°F. The most important of these two is the RH, but if the temperature varies, as the air expands or contracts, then so too does the RH, so for this reason it is important to control the temperature. One has to aim to keep the temperature in a humidor as constant as possible, and then use the humidifier to compensate for the background fluctuations in the weather and ambient RH. When the ambient RH falls it is apt to drag down the RH in your humidor, so be sensitive to the weather and to the condition of your cigars.

However it is not enough to simply maintain the correct RH and temperature in a humidor; for optimum storage cigars need fresh moist air, not stagnant moist air, so one needs to ensure that air circulates around the cigars for best results. Humidors designed without air holes need to be opened frequently enough to prevent the atmosphere within from going stale.

It is quite common to hear people keeping their cigars in the fridge in the absence of a humidor. This practice should be thoroughly discouraged, for not only is a fridge too dry and cold (you only have to look at a piece of lettuce that has been left in the fridge) but also is full of strong odors of foods that cigars should not be allowed anywhere near. There is no benefit in keeping cigars in a fridge, and people are better off keeping them in a cedar box placed in a plastic bag with a little moisture sprayed in and then stored somewhere away from dry heat, cold, and strong odors.

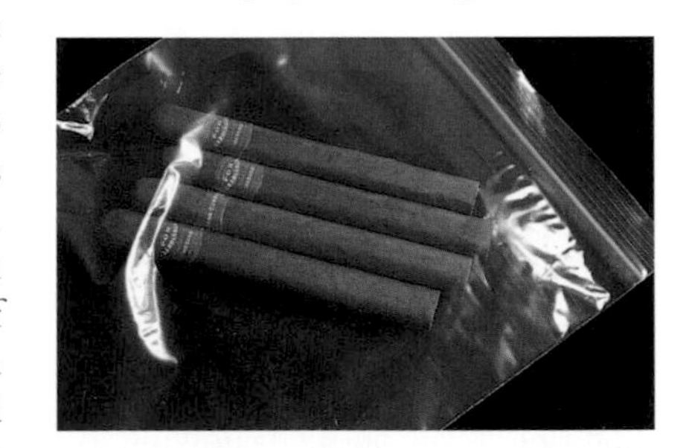
AS A LAST RESORT A PLASTIC BAG CAN BE USED TO PREVENT CIGARS FROM DRYING OUT.

RECONDITIONING CIGARS

Cigars that are too moist will feel soggy and, given enough time in this state, will start producing an excessive amount of bloom that looks like white mold on the wrapper. If this state is allowed to continue for too long the cigars will rot and then be beyond help. However if you intervene in good time you need only to brush off the bloom, leave the humidor open for a while in order that it and the cigars dry out a bit, and readjust down the level at which your humidification unit is set.

Cigars that have become too dry need only be put into a well functioning humidor for a month or so and in this time they will slowly absorb moisture and return to condition. However cigars that have spent too long in a hot dry place may have "died" and no re-moisturizing will save them.

ENJOYING A PREMIUM CIGAR

CUTTING

Because most premium cigars have the mouth end sealed with a cap of tobacco you have to create an opening in the head of the cigar before you can smoke it. So where exactly does one do this and with what?

A good sharp guillotine or pair of cigar scissors do the job very well and are recommendable. V-Cutters can be quite awkward to use as often they do not fit the cigar being cut, or are not sharp enough and more tear their way through the cap than cut it. Piercing, with a match or anything else, is to be positively discouraged as it can upset the way the filler leaves guide the smoke and result in a focus for heat and tars. Using your own fingernails or teeth is fine, but only if you know what you are doing; with this natural method the risks of removing the whole cap and then standing by helpless as the wrapper unravels are great.

REMOVING PART OF THE CAP FROM THE HEAD OF A CIGAR USING CIGAR SCISSORS.

Assuming that a guillotine is used, then where is the best place to cut? The cap that is used to seal the cigar also keeps the wrapper leaf from unraveling, so it is important when cutting to leave enough of the cap in place to ensure this does not happen, whilst at the same time opening up the cigar to the full extent of its bore so that one can draw freely from it. Therefore the best place to cut is right on the shoulders of the cigar, removing the top of the cap as if it were a thin layer of skin but not cutting too deeply into the body of the cigar.

THE BAND

Taking the band off a cigar often risks damaging the wrapper as the two are sometimes glued together. If you wish to take the band off, this can usually be done without damaging the wrapper after one third of the cigar has been smoked, for by then the wrapper has warmed up and become more subtle. Even then the band should not be pulled off, like a ring off a finger, but rather peeled off.

LIGHTING

Lighting is all about following two simple rules; take your time, and do a thorough job. The worst thing that can happen is a partial lighting, as then the cigar burns down unevenly and does not draw well. An even ignition must be achieved before the smoker settles down to enjoy the cigar.

The best route to an even ignition is to first of all char the end of the cigar, holding it at forty-five percent to the flame to avoid scorch marks to the wrapper. This charring leaves the cigar ready to catch at the next stage, which is when the smoker puts the cigar to the mouth, draws on it whilst rotating it just above the flame, and causes the flame to "jump" on to the end of the cigar. A blow on the lit end will show how thorough an ignition has taken place, and if necessary the cigar is returned to the flame and drawn on until the entire end of the cigar has caught.

LIGHTING A CIGAR. DO A THOROUGH JOB.

It is very important that an odorless flame be used to light a cigar. This means that wooden matches and butane lighters are good for the job, whilst petrol lighters and candles are bad; the dirty odors from these last two will be drawn through the cigar and interfere with its natural tobacco flavors.

Smoking

To best enjoy a cigar one should not inhale the smoke. The true pleasure is to be found in appreciating the composition of tobacco flavors and these can only be detected on the palate by your sense of taste. Thus any smoke inhaled to the toes is wasted.

What to do with the ash of the cigar is a consideration worth mentioning. Many first time smokers will be tempted to treat their cigar like a cigarette—continually tapping the slightest ash off—when in fact a cigar's ash should be allowed to build up until it is ready to fall, as its consistency is a testimony to how well the cigar has been made.

Cigars often go out in the course of being smoked, especially as they near the last third. This is because natural oils are concentrating in the reducing cigar, and they automatically put the cigar out if it is not being drawn on regularly. This does not necessarily mean that the cigar is finished, but probably that it is time to re-light. As a rule of thumb you can re-light a cigar up to an hour after it has gone out without its flavors deteriorating. Half-smoked cigars cannot be left for finishing the following day, as the cigar goes stale in the meantime and is not pleasant on re-lighting.

Re-lighting

Re-lighting can be done in an easy way and a hard way: The hard way is to put the cigar to your lips, apply a flame, and start drawing. Thirty seconds later you could still be drawing and most certainly will be getting short of breath. The easy way is to clean the end of the cigar of ash by rolling it in an ashtray, char it for a period of time (taking your time once again), and then raise the cigar to your lips and draw. In all probability the cigar will burst back to life, as its oils have heated up sufficiently to rekindle the fire. If not, all that remains to be done is a few seconds drawing on the cigar whilst applying the flame, and an almost effortless ignition will take place.

Parting company

If a cigar is not necessarily finished when it goes out, then how does one know when to part company with it? Some say that as you reach the last third of the cigar you have had the best and should graciously accept that the pleasure of smoking is over, for the time being at least. This claim is based on the fact that the further down the cigar you smoke, the richer—some say stronger—it becomes. This can be explained by the way that it has been constructed, with the lightest end of the leaf situated at the cigar's foot, becoming increasingly stronger as you travel down the cigar, to the strongest part of the leaf—that which was attached to the stem of the plant—at the head of the cigar. As you near the end, the richer is the part of the leaf being smoked. So in other words what they are saying is that you should quit while you are ahead and not risk smoking on until you meet an aggressive aftertaste. However, as everyone's tastes are different, I recommend that you smoke to the point where you feel you are ready to put down the cigar; for one person this might be at the start of the last third, but for another it might be when burning fingers and lips warn that there is nothing left of the cigar to smoke. Each to their own is the best guide here.

When the time comes to part with the cigar it is not necessary to stub it out like a cigarette for this is likely to end in a mess and lots of smoke. All you need do is lay it to rest in an ashtray, and the cigar will quickly put itself out.

PART II

The Cigar Directory

INTRODUCTION TO THE DIRECTORY

The directory uses the following scales of assessment:

FLAVOR	QUALITY
Mild	Poor
Mild to medium	Average
Medium	Good
Medium to full	Excellent
Full	Outstanding

The directory features 115 of the premium cigar brands on sale in the world today, and gives you what I call the "vital statistics" of each—where it is made, the provenance of its filler, binder, and wrapper leaves, and a listing of all the cigar sizes and names that form its line.

In preparing for this book I was only able to smoke one cigar from each brand, based on which I write a few words by way of comment on each cigar's character and quality. With so many brands to include it was just not possible to smoke more, and yet tasting a single cigar is little evidence upon which to judge a whole brand. Essentially therefore, my comments must be understood as relating to the sample cigar and not to the entire brand. Having said this, however, in one respect a brand is only as good as each cigar made in its name.

At no point in the directory do I mention prices, but I would ask the reader to bear them in mind. As there are considerable price differentials between brands it is unfair to compare them as if they were all equal, and I recognize that one of this directory's shortcomings is its failure to point you in the direction of value for money.

Readers should know that I work at Hunters & Frankau, importers of Havanas and other fine cigar brands to the United Kingdom, and it is very possible that my familiarity with our brands has influenced my preferences. So, when reading my comments in the directory keep the following observation in mind; *"Sobre gusto no hay nada escrito"*—the old Spanish adage which roughly translates as "When it comes to tastes nothing is etched in stone." What suits me may not suit you.

ALIADOS

CTRY OF MANU	HONDURAS
FILLER	BRAZIL/DOMINICAN REPUBLIC
BINDER	ECUADOR
WRAPPER	ECUADOR
FLAVOR	MEDIUM TO FULL
QUALITY	EXCELLENT
COMMENT	RICH AND EARTHY, WITH A WELL-BALANCED CHORUS OF TOBACCO FLAVORS

VITOLAS

NAME	LENGTH	RING GAUGE
General	18in	66
Figurin	10in	60
Diamedas	7½in	60
Piramides	7½in	60
Churchill	7¼in	54
Valentino	7in	48
Cazadore	7in	45
Palma	7in	36
Corona Deluxe	6½in	45
Fuma	6½in	45
Lonsdale	6½in	42
Toro	6in	54
No.4	5½in	45
Remedios	5½in	42
Rothschild	5in	51
Petit Cetro	5in	36

CORONA DELUXE/6½IN/RING GAUGE 45

ANDUJAR

CTRY OF MANU	DOMINICAN REPUBLIC
FILLER	DOMINICAN REPUBLIC
BINDER	DOMINICAN REPUBLIC
WRAPPER	CONNECTICUT
FLAVOR	MILD
QUALITY	AVERAGE
COMMENT	NOT A GOOD-LOOKING CIGAR, STARTING GRASSY AND GREEN, BUT IMPROVING TO BETTER BALANCE WITH A BIT OF SWEETNESS

VITOLAS

NAME	LENGTH	RING GAUGE
Azua	9in	46
Santiago	7½in	50
Macorix	6½in	44
Samana	6in	38
Vega	5in	50
Romano	5in	25

VEGA/5IN/RING GAUGE 50

ARTURO FUENTE

CTRY OF MANU	DOMINICAN REPUBLIC
FILLER	DOMINICAN REPUBLIC
BINDER	DOMINICAN REPUBLIC
WRAPPER	CAMEROON
FLAVOR	MEDIUM
QUALITY	OUTSTANDING
COMMENT	A HANDSOME LOOKING CIGAR WITH A GOOD DRAW. LOVELY CLEAN FLAVORS WITH SPICE BUT NO HEAVINESS

VITOLAS

NAME	LENGTH	RING GAUGE
Canones	8½in	52
Royal Salute	7⅝in	52
Churchill	7½in	48
Panetela Fina	7in	38
Double Corona	6¾in	48
Privada No.1	6¾in	46
Lonsdale	6½in	42
Flor Fina	6in	46
Cuban Corona	5¼in	44
Petit Corona	5in	38
Chateau Fuente	4½in	50

CUBAN CORONA/5¼IN/RING GAUGE 44

ARTURO FUENTE CIGARS

ASHTON

Ctry of Manu	Dominican Republic
Filler	Dominican Republic
Binder	Dominican Republic
Wrapper	Connecticut
Flavor	Mild to medium
Quality	Excellent
Comment	Smokes beautifully, with soft but spicy flavors

Vitolas

Name	Length	Ring Gauge
Churchill	7½in	52
Prime Minister	6⅞in	48
8-9-8	6½in	44
Corona	5½in	44
Panetela	6in	36
Magnum	5in	50
Cordial	5in	30

Churchill/7½in/Ring Gauge 52

ASTRAL

Ctry of Manu	Honduras
Filler	Honduras/Nicaragua
Binder	Honduras
Wrapper	Honduras
Flavor	Mild
Quality	Excellent
Comment	Smokes very well, offering soft and delicate tobacco flavors with a sweet edge

Vitolas

Name	Length	Ring Gauge
Maestro	7½in	52
Favorito	7in	48
Perfeccion	7in	48
Lujos	6½in	44
Besos	5in	52

Lujos/6½in/Ring Gauge 44

AVO

Ctry of Manu	Dominican Republic
Filler	Dominican Republic
Binder	Dominican Republic
Wrapper	Connecticut
Flavor	Medium to full
Quality	Good
Comment	Big tobacco flavors that, though pleasant, somewhat lack finesse

Vitolas

Name	Length	Ring Gauge
Avo No.3	7½in	52
Avo No.4	7in	38
Pyramid	7in	36/54
Avo No.5	6¾in	46
Avo No.1	6¾in	42
Avo No.6	6½in	36
Belicoso	6in	50
Avo No.2	6in	50
Avo No.7	6in	44
Avo No.8	5½in	40
Petit Belicoso	4¾in	50
Avo No.9	4¾in	48

No.2/6in/Ring Gauge 50

AVO XO

CTRY OF MANU	DOMINICAN REPUBLIC
FILLER	DOMINICAN REPUBLIC
BINDER	DOMINICAN REPUBLIC
WRAPPER	CONNECTICUT
FLAVOR	MILD TO MEDIUM
QUALITY	EXCELLENT
COMMENT	COMPLEX AND DELICIOUS, WITH A SOFT SWEET CHARACTER. PLEASANT TO THE END

VITOLAS

NAME	LENGTH	RING GAUGE
Maestoso	7in	48
Preludio	6in	40
Intermezzo	5½in	50

MAESTOSO/7IN/RING GAUGE 48

BACCARAT

CTRY OF MANU	HONDURAS
FILLER	HONDURAS
BINDER	MEXICO
WRAPPER	HONDURAS
FLAVOR	FULL
QUALITY	AVERAGE
COMMENT	CONSTRUCTION FAULTS EMERGED DURING SMOKING. SALTY TOBACCO WAS THE OVERRIDING FLAVOR

VITOLAS

NAME	LENGTH	RING GAUGE
Polo	7in	52
Churchill	7in	50
No.1	7in	44
Luchadore	6in	43
Panatela	6in	38
Petit Corona	5½in	42
Rothschild	5in	50
Platinum	4⅞in	32
Bonitas	4½in	30

POLO/7IN/RING GAUGE 52

BACCARAT CIGARS

BAHIA

Ctry of Manu	Costa Rica
Filler	Nicaragua
Binder	Nicaragua
Wrapper	Ecuador
Flavor	Medium to full
Quality	Average
Comment	A meaty smoke of thick tobacco flavors but short of elegance

Vitolas

Name	Length	Ring Gauge
Double Coronas	8in	50
Churchills	6⅞in	48
Esplendidos	6in	50
No.3	6in	46
No.4	5½in	42
Robusto	5in	50

No.3/6in/Ring Gauge 46

BANCES

Ctry of Manu	Honduras
Filler	Honduras/Nicaragua/Dominican Republic
Binder	Honduras
Wrapper	Ecuador
Flavor	Medium
Quality	Good
Comment	Thick tobacco flavors with an oily edge. Pleasant albeit lacking sophistication

Vitolas

Name	Length	Ring Gauge
President	8½in	52
Corona Inmensas	6¾in	48
No.1	6½in	43
Cazadores	6¼in	44
Breva	5¼in	43

Cazadores/6¼in/Ring Gauge 44

BAUZA

Ctry of Manu	Dominican Republic
Filler	Dominican Republic/Nicaragua
Binder	Mexico
Wrapper	Ecuador
Flavor	Medium
Quality	Excellent
Comment	Deep tobacco flavors flecked with dark chocolate and coffee

Vitolas

Name	Length	Ring Gauge
Fabulosos	7½in	50
Medalla D'Oro No.1	6⅞in	44
Florete	6⅞in	35
Casa Grande	6¾in	48
Jaguar	6½in	42
Robusto	5½in	50
Grecos	5½in	42
Petit Corona	5in	38

Jaguar/6½in/Ring Gauge 42

BELINDA

CTRY OF MANU	HONDURAS
FILLER	DOMINICAN REPUBLIC/ HONDURAS
BINDER	HONDURAS
WRAPPER	CONNECTICUT/ECUADOR/ HONDURAS
FLAVOR	MEDIUM
QUALITY	GOOD
COMMENT	PLEASANT AND STRAIGHTFORWARD TOBACCO FLAVORS WITH A SLIGHT WOODNINESS

VITOLAS

NAME	LENGTH	RING GAUGE
Prime Minister	7½in	50
Ramon	7¼in	47
Belinda	6½in	36
Corona Grande	6¼in	44
Spanish Twist	6¼in	43
Excellente	6in	50
Cabinet	5⅝in	45
Breva Conserva	5½in	43
Mina	5⅜in	28
Dina	5in	36
Madaglia D'Oro	4½in	50
Robusto en Cedro	4½in	50
Petit Corona	5in	38

BREVA CONSERVA/5½IN/RING GAUGE 43

BERING

CTRY OF MANU	HONDURAS
FILLER	HONDURAS/MEXICO/DOMINICAN REPUBLIC/NICARAGUA
BINDER	HONDURAS
WRAPPER	CONNECTICUT
FLAVOR	MILD
QUALITY	AVERAGE
COMMENT	SADLY A MEAN DRAW SABOTAGED THE FLAVORS OF THIS CIGAR MAKING IT APPEAR THIN

VITOLAS

NAME	LENGTH	RING GAUGE
Grande	8½in	52
Barons	7¼in	42
Inmensas	7⅛in	45
Casinos	7⅛in	42
Torpedo	7in	31/54
Corona Grande	6¼in	46
Cazadores	6¼in	45
Gold No.1	6¼in	33
Hispanos	6in	50
Plaza	6in	43
Natural	6in	41
Imperiales	5¼in	42
Coronados	5$\frac{3}{16}$in	45
Robusto	4¾in	50

IMPERIAL/5¼IN/RING GAUGE 42

A VARIETY OF BERING CIGARS

BOLIVAR

CTRY OF MANU	CUBA
FILLER	CUBA
BINDER	CUBA
WRAPPER	CUBA
FLAVOR	FULL
QUALITY	EXCELLENT
COMMENT	A VERY RICH AND ELEGANT BLEND OF TOBACCO FLAVORS

VITOLAS

NAME	LENGTH	RING GAUGE
Coronas Gigantes	7in	47
Palmas	7in	33
Inmensas	6⅝in	43
Gold Medal	6⅜in	42
Coronas Extras	5⅝in	44
Belicosos Finos	5½in	52
Coronas	5½in	42
Petit Coronas	5in	42
Bonitas	5in	40
Royal Coronas	4⅞in	50
Coronas Junior	4¼in	42

CORONA JUNIOR/4¼IN/RING GAUGE 42

BOLIVAR CIGARS

CABALLEROS

CTRY OF MANU	DOMINICAN REPUBLIC
FILLER	DOMINICAN REPUBLIC
BINDER	DOMINICAN REPUBLIC
WRAPPER	CONNECTICUT
FLAVOR	MILD
QUALITY	GOOD
COMMENT	MILD AND CREAMY TOBACCO FLAVORS IDEALLY SUITED TO THE MORNING

VITOLAS

NAME	LENGTH	RING GAUGE
Churchill	7in	50
Double Corona	6¾in	48
Lonsdale	6½in	42
Corona	5¾in	43
Petit Corona	5½in	42
Rothschild	5in	50

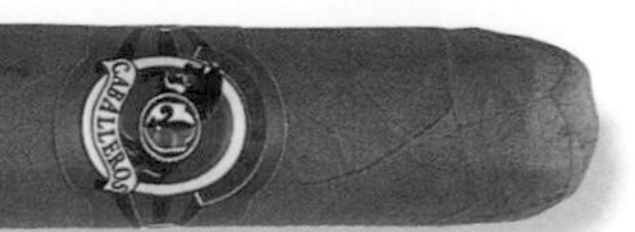

CHURCHILL/7IN/RING GAUGE 50

CALIXTO LOPEZ

Ctry of Manu	Indonesia/Java
Filler	Philippines
Binder	Philippines
Wrapper	Philippines
Flavor	Medium
Quality	Average
Comment	Construction faults emerged during smoking. Somewhat muddy flavors

Vitolas

Name	Length	Ring Gauge
Gigantes	8½in	50
Czar	8in	45
Palma	7⅛in	36
Lonsdale	6¾in	42
Nobles	6½in	50
No.1	6⅜in	45
Corona	5⅜in	43

Corona/5⅜in/Ring Gauge 43

Calixto Lopez cigars

CANARIO D'ORO

Ctry of Manu	Dominican Republic
Filler	Dominican Republic
Binder	Dominican Republic
Wrapper	Cameroon
Flavor	Medium
Quality	Good
Comment	Well-constructed with straightforward tobacco flavors

Vitolas

Name	Length	Ring Gauge
Supremos	7in	45
Lonsdale	6½in	42
Vista	6¼in	32
Fino	6in	31
Immensos	5½in	49
Corona	5½in	42
Rothschild	4½in	50
Babies	4¼in	32

Immensos/5½in/Ring Gauge 49

C.A.O.

CTRY OF MANU	HONDURAS
FILLER	NICARAGUA/MEXICO
BINDER	HONDURAS
WRAPPER	CONNECTICUT
FLAVOR	MILD
QUALITY	GOOD
COMMENT	WELL-CONSTRUCTED WITH AN EXCELLENT DRAW. SMOOTH, AND A BIT SWEET, ALTHOUGH SLIGHTLY UNIMAGINATIVE

VITOLAS

NAME	LENGTH	RING GAUGE
Churchill	8in	50
Presidente	7½in	54
Triangualre	7in	36/54
Lonsdale	7in	44
Corona Gorda	6in	50
Corona	6in	42
Petit Corona	5in	40
Robusto	4½in	50
Maduro		
Churchill	8in	50
Presidente	7½in	54
Triangulare	7in	36/54
Corona Gorda	6in	50
Corona	6in	42
Robusto	4½in	50

PRESIDENTE/7½IN/RING GAUGE 54

C.A.O. GOLD

CTRY OF MANU	NICARAGUA
FILLER	NICARAGUA
BINDER	NICARAGUA
WRAPPER	ECUADOR
FLAVOR	MILD TO MEDIUM
QUALITY	AVERAGE
COMMENT	WELL-CONSTRUCTED, STARTING OFF MILD AND PLEASANT, BUT BECOMING A BIT SOUR IN THE SECOND HALF

VITOLAS

NAME	LENGTH	RING GAUGE
Double Corona	7½in	54
Churchill	7in	48
Corona Gorda	6½in	50
Corona	5½in	42
Robusto	5in	50

CORONA GORDA/6½IN/RING GAUGE 50

CARLIN

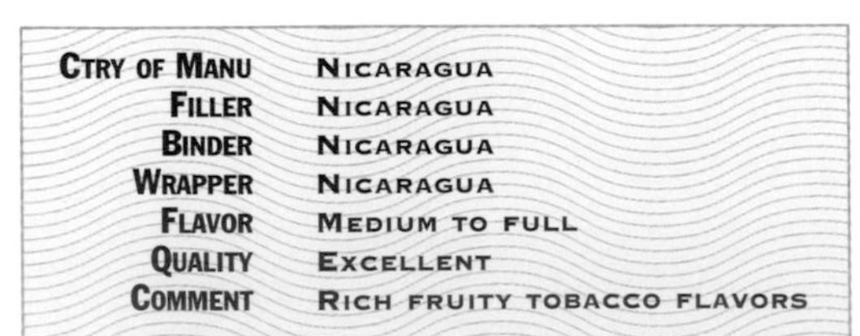

CTRY OF MANU	NICARAGUA
FILLER	NICARAGUA
BINDER	NICARAGUA
WRAPPER	NICARAGUA
FLAVOR	MEDIUM TO FULL
QUALITY	EXCELLENT
COMMENT	RICH FRUITY TOBACCO FLAVORS

VITOLAS

NAME	LENGTH	RING GAUGE
Gigante	8in	52
Churchill	7in	48
Toro	6in	50
Corona	5½in	43
Robusto	4¾in	52

TORO/6IN/RING GAUGE 50

CARLOS TORANO

CTRY OF MANU	DOMINICAN REPUBLIC
FILLER	DOMINICAN REPUBLIC
BINDER	DOMINICAN REPUBLIC
WRAPPER	CONNECTICUT
FLAVOR	MILD
QUALITY	AVERAGE
COMMENT	VERY MILD AND WITH LITTLE AFTERTASTE

VITOLAS

NAME	LENGTH	RING GAUGE
Carlos III	7½in	52
Carlos VI	7in	48
Carlos II	6¾in	43
Carlos VIII	6½in	36
Carlos I	6in	50
Carlos V	6in	46
Carlos IV	5¾in	43
Carlos VII	4¾in	52

CARLOS II/6¾IN/RING GAUGE 43

CASA BLANCA

CTRY OF MANU	DOMINICAN REPUBLIC
FILLER	DOMINICAN REPUBLIC
BINDER	MEXICO
WRAPPER	CONNECTICUT
FLAVOR	MILD
QUALITY	EXCELLENT
COMMENT	A SOFT BLEND OF TOBACCO FLAVORS, WELL SUITED TO THE MORNING

VITOLAS

NAME	LENGTH	RING GAUGE
Jeroboam	10in	66
Presidente	7½in	50
Magnum	7in	60
Lonsdale	6½in	42
Panatela	6in	35
DeLuxe	6in	50
Corona	5½in	42
Half Jeroboam	5in	66
Bonita	4in	36

LONSDALE/6½IN/RING GAUGE 42

V CENTENNIAL

CTRY OF MANU	HONDURAS
FILLER	HONDURAS/NICARAGUA/ DOMINICAN REPUBLIC
BINDER	MEXICO
WRAPPER	CONNECTICUT
FLAVOR	MEDIUM TO FULL
QUALITY	EXCELLENT
COMMENT	COMPLEX AND RICH SPICY FLAVORS

VITOLAS

NAME	LENGTH	RING GAUGE
Presidente	8in	50
Numero Uno	7½in	38
Torpedo	7in	54
Churchill	7in	48
Cetro	6¼in	44
Numero Dos	6in	50
Coronas	5½in	42
Robusto	5in	50

CETRO/6¼IN/RING GAUGE 44

COHIBA

CTRY OF MANU	CUBA
FILLER	CUBA
BINDER	CUBA
WRAPPER	CUBA
FLAVOR	MEDIUM TO FULL
QUALITY	OUTSTANDING
COMMENT	RICH, REFINED, AND EXCITING, WITH GREAT ELEGANCE

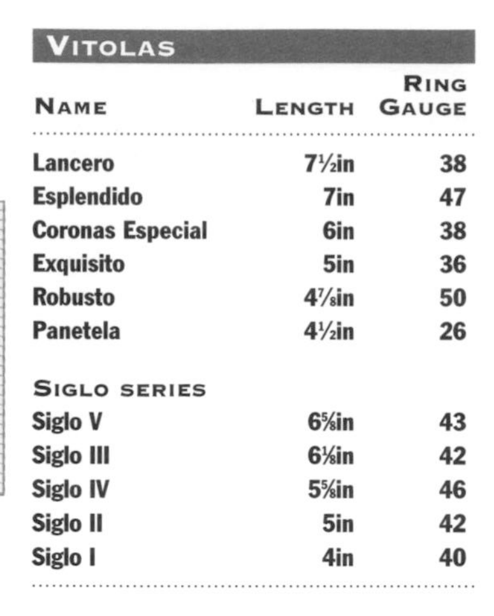

VITOLAS

NAME	LENGTH	RING GAUGE
Lancero	7½in	38
Esplendido	7in	47
Coronas Especial	6in	38
Exquisito	5in	36
Robusto	4⅞in	50
Panetela	4½in	26
SIGLO SERIES		
Siglo V	6⅝in	43
Siglo III	6⅛in	42
Siglo IV	5⅝in	46
Siglo II	5in	42
Siglo I	4in	40

A CUBAN COHIBA CIGAR BOX

LANCERO/7½IN/RING GAUGE 38

ROBUSTO/4⅞IN/RING GAUGE 50

ESPLENDIDO/7IN/RING GAUGE 47

CREDO

CTRY OF MANU	DOMINICAN REPUBLIC
FILLER	DOMINICAN REPUBLIC
BINDER	DOMINICAN REPUBLIC
WRAPPER	CONNECTICUT
FLAVOR	MILD
QUALITY	POOR
COMMENT	ALTHOUGH WELL-CONSTRUCTED, A BLAND SMOKING EXPERIENCE

VITOLAS

NAME	LENGTH	RING GAUGE
Magnificat	6⅞in	46
Anthanor	5¾in	42
Pythagoras	5in	50
Jubilate	5in	34

MAGNIFICAT/6⅞IN/RING GAUGE 46

CRUZ REAL

CTRY OF MANU	MEXICO
FILLER	MEXICO
BINDER	MEXICO
WRAPPER	MEXICO
FLAVOR	MEDIUM TO FULL
QUALITY	GOOD
COMMENT	PLEASANT TOBACCO FLAVORS WITH A BIT OF SWEETNESS BUT LACKING IN COMPLEXITY

VITOLAS

NAME	LENGTH	RING GAUGE
No.28	8½in	54
No.14	7½in	50
No.1	6⅝in	42
No.3	6⅝in	36
No.19	6in	50
No.2	6in	42
No.25	5½in	52
No.24	4½in	50

NO.2/6IN/RING GAUGE 42

CUABA

CTRY OF MANU	CUBA
FILLER	CUBA
BINDER	CUBA
WRAPPER	CUBA
FLAVOR	MEDIUM TO FULL
QUALITY	OUTSTANDING
COMMENT	THE FIRST FEW PUFFS ARE REMARKABLE AS THEY CONSIST ALMOST ENTIRELY OF THE FLAVOR OF THE WRAPPER. ONCE INTO THE FULL BLEND THE FLAVOR IS CHARMING

VITOLAS

NAME	LENGTH	RING GAUGE
Exclusivos	5⅝in	46
Generosos	5¼in	42
Tradicionales	4¾in	42
Divinos	4in	43

TRADICIONALES/4¾IN/RING GAUGE 42

CUESTA-REY

CTRY OF MANU	DOMINICAN REPUBLIC
FILLER	DOMINICAN REPUBLIC
BINDER	DOMINICAN REPUBLIC
WRAPPER	CONNECTICUT
FLAVOR	MILD TO MEDIUM
QUALITY	EXCELLENT
COMMENT	WELL-BALANCED WITH CAFE-AU-LAIT STYLE TOBACCO FLAVORS

VITOLAS

NAME	LENGTH	RING GAUGE
Dominican No.1	8½in	52
Individual	8½in	52
Dominican No.2	7¼in	48
Aristocrat	7¼in	48
Dominican No.3	7in	36
Riviera	7in	35
Dominican No.4	6½in	42
Captiva	6³⁄₁₆in	42
Dominican No.60	6in	50
Dominican No.5	5½in	43
Robusto	4½in	50
Cameo-Imported	4¼in	32

ROBUSTO/4½IN/RING GAUGE 50

DAVIDOFF

CTRY OF MANU	DOMINICAN REPUBLIC
FILLER	DOMINICAN REPUBLIC
BINDER	DOMINICAN REPUBLIC
WRAPPER	CONNECTICUT
FLAVOR	MILD TO MEDIUM
QUALITY	OUTSTANDING
COMMENT	GENEROUS DRAW GIVING PLEASING FLAVORS WITH A SUGGESTION OF MINT. DEVELOPS IN DEPTH WITH A LONG AFTERTASTE

VITOLAS

NAME	LENGTH	RING GAUGE
Aniversario No.1	$8\frac{2}{3}$in	48
Double R	$7\frac{1}{2}$in	50
Davidoff No.1	$7\frac{1}{2}$in	38
Aniversario No.2	7in	48
3000	7in	33
Grand Cru No.1	$6\frac{3}{32}$in	42
4000	$6\frac{3}{32}$in	42
Special T	6in	52
Davidoff No.2	6in	38
Davidoff Tubos	6in	38
5000	$5\frac{5}{8}$in	46
Grand Cru No.2	$5\frac{5}{8}$in	42
Davidoff No.3	$5\frac{1}{8}$in	30
Grand Cru No.3	5in	42
2000	5in	42
Special R	$4\frac{7}{8}$in	50
Grand Cru No.4	$4\frac{5}{8}$in	40
1000	$4\frac{5}{8}$in	34
Ambassadrice	$4\frac{5}{8}$in	26
Grand Cru No.5	4in	40

GRAND CRU NO.1/$6\frac{3}{32}$IN/RING GAUGE 42

SPECIAL R/$4\frac{7}{8}$IN/RING GAUGE 50

DAVIDOFF CIGARS

DIPLOMATICOS

CTRY OF MANU	CUBA
FILLER	CUBA
BINDER	CUBA
WRAPPER	CUBA
FLAVOR	MEDIUM TOF FULL
QUALITY	EXCELLENT
COMMENT	WELL-CONSTRUCTED, WITH A RICH BUT SUBTLE FLAVOR AND EXCELLENT AROMA

VITOLAS

NAME	LENGTH	RING GAUGE
No.6	$7\frac{1}{2}$in	38
No.1	$6\frac{1}{2}$in	42
No.2	$6\frac{1}{8}$in	52
No.7	6in	38
No.3	$5\frac{1}{2}$in	42
No.4	5in	42
No.5	4in	40

NO.7/6IN/RING GAUGE 38

DON DIEGO

CTRY OF MANU	DOMINICAN REPUBLIC
FILLER	DOMINICAN REPUBLIC
BINDER	DOMINICAN REPUBLIC
WRAPPER	CONNECTICUT
FLAVOR	MILD TO MEDIUM
QUALITY	EXCELLENT
COMMENT	GOOD DRAW AND BURN, WITH NUTTY TOBACCO FLAVORS AND A SWEET UNDERCURRENT

VITOLAS

NAME	LENGTH	RING GAUGE
Monarch Tubes	7¼in	46
Lonsdales	6⅝in	42
Coronas Bravas	6½in	48
Grecos	6½in	38
Royal Palms Tubes	6⅛in	36
Coronas	5⅝in	42
Petit Corona	5⅛in	42
Corona Major Tubes	5¹⁄₁₆in	42
Babies	5¹⁄₁₆in	33
Preludes	4in	28

CORONA/5⅝IN/RING GAUGE 42

DON DIEGO CIGARS

DON LINO

CTRY OF MANU	HONDURAS
FILLER	HONDURAS
BINDER	HONDURAS
WRAPPER	CONNECTICUT/CAMEROON
FLAVOR	MEDIUM TO FULL
QUALITY	EXCELLENT
COMMENT	SPICY RICH TOBACCO FLAVORS WITH COMPLEXITY

VITOLAS

NAME	LENGTH	RING GAUGE
Supremos	8½in	52
Churchill	7½in	48
Torpedo	7in	50
Panetelas	7in	36
Tubos	6½in	44
No.1	6½in	44
No.5	6¼in	44
No.3	6in	36
Corona	5½in	50
Robusto	5½in	50
Toros	5½in	46
Petitcetro	5½in	42
No.4	5in	42
Rothschild	4½in	50
Epicure	4½in	32

NO.4/5IN/RING GAUGE 42

DON MATEO

CTRY OF MANU	HONDURAS
FILLER	NICARAGUA
BINDER	MEXICO
WRAPPER	MEXICO
FLAVOR	MEDIUM
QUALITY	AVERAGE
COMMENT	PEPPERY AND GRAINY TOBACCO FLAVORS

VITOLAS

NAME	LENGTH	RING GAUGE
No.10	8in	52
No.9	7½in	50
No.1	7in	30
No.6	6⅞in	48
No.2	6⅞in	35
No.11	6⅝in	54
No.5	6⅝in	44
No.8	6¼in	50
No.3	6in	42
No.4	5½in	44
No.7	4¾in	50

No.9/7½in/Ring Gauge 50

DON PEPE

CTRY OF MANU	BRAZIL
FILLER	BRAZIL
BINDER	BRAZIL
WRAPPER	BRAZIL
FLAVOR	MEDIUM TO FULL
QUALITY	EXCELLENT
COMMENT	A MEATY SMOKE THAT IS RICH AND EARTHY

VITOLAS

NAME	LENGTH	RING GAUGE
Double Corona	7½in	52
Churchill	7in	48
Petit Lonsdale	6in	43
Slim Panatela	5¼in	26
Robusto	5in	52
Half Corona	4¼in	34

Churchill/7in/Ring Gauge 48

DON RAMOS

CTRY OF MANU	HONDURAS
FILLER	HONDURAS
BINDER	HONDURAS
WRAPPER	CONNECTICUT
FLAVOR	FULL
QUALITY	EXCELLENT
COMMENT	FULL-FLAVORED WITH A SPICY RICHNESS

VITOLAS

NAME	LENGTH	RING GAUGE
No.11	6¾in	47
No.13	5⅝in	46
No.14	5½in	42
No.16	5in	42
No.20	4½in	52
No.19	4½in	50
No.17	4in	42

No.14/5½in/Ring Gauge 42

DON TOMAS

CTRY OF MANU	HONDURAS
FILLER	HONDURAS
BINDER	HONDURAS
WRAPPER	HONDURAS
FLAVOR	MEDIUM
QUALITY	GOOD
COMMENT	A GOOD DRAW BEARING A PLEASING COLLECTION OF FLAVORS INCLUDING ROAST NUTS AND SPICE

VITOLAS

NAME	LENGTH	RING GAUGE
Gigantes	8½in	52
Imperiales No.1	8in	44
Presidentes	7½in	50
Panatela Largas	7in	38
Corona Grandes	6½in	44
Cetros No.2	6½in	44
Supremos	6¼in	42
Panatelas	6in	36
Coronas	5½in	50
Toros	5½in	46
Matadors	5½in	42
Blunts	5in	42
Rothschild	4½in	50
Epicures	4½in	32
SPECIAL EDITION		
No.100	7½in	50
No.400	7in	36
No.200	6½in	44
No.500	5½in	46
No.300	5in	50

CORONA GRANDE/6½IN/RING GAUGE 44

DON TOMAS CIGARS

DUNHILL

CTRY OF MANU	CANARY ISLES
FILLER	BRAZIL/DOMINICAN REPUBLIC
BINDER	DOMINICAN REPUBLIC
WRAPPER	CONNECTICUT
FLAVOR	MILD
QUALITY	GOOD
COMMENT	A VERY LIGHT SMOKE WITH A TOUCH OF SWEETNESS

VITOLAS

NAME	LENGTH	RING GAUGE
Lonsdale Grandes	7½in	42
Corona Grandes	6½in	43
Panatelas	6in	30
Corona Extra	5½in	50
Coronas	5½in	43

CORONA EXTRA/5½IN/RING GAUGE 50

DUNHILL

Ctry of Manu	Dominican Republica
Filler	Brazil/Dominican Republic
Binder	Dominican Republic
Wrapper	Connecticut
Flavor	Mild
Quality	Excellent
Comment	A very good draw providing well-balanced tobacco flavors

Vitolas

Name	Length	Ring Gauge
Peravias	7in	50
Cabreras	7in	48
Fantinos	7in	28
Diamantes	6⅝in	42
Samanas	6½in	38
Centenas	6in	50
Condados	6in	48
Tabaras	5 9/16in	42
Valverdes	5 9/16in	42
Altamiras	5in	48
Romanas	4½in	50
Bavaros	4½in	28
Caletas	4in	42

Romanas/4½in/Ring Gauge 50

EL REY DEL MUNDO

Ctry of Manu	Cuba
Filler	Cuba
Binder	Cuba
Wrapper	Cuba
Flavor	Mild
Quality	Excellent
Comment	Hints of chocolate orange in a smoke of charming flavors

Vitolas

Name	Length	Ring Gauge
Tainos	7in	47
Lonsdales	6⅜in	42
Gran Corona	5½in	46
Isabel	5½in	43
Coronas de Luxe	5½in	42
Choix Supreme	5in	49
Petit Coronas	5in	42
Demi-Tasse	4in	30
Demi-Tasse	3⅞in	30

Choix Supreme/5in/Ring Gauge 48

El Rey del Mundo cigars

EL REY DEL MUNDO

Ctry of Manu	Honduras
Filler	Honduras
Binder	Honduras
Wrapper	Ecuador
Flavor	Full
Quality	Excellent
Comment	An espresso character with flavors that are thick, syrupy, and tasty

Vitolas

Name	Length	Ring Gauge
Coronation	8½in	52
Principale	8in	47
Flor del Mundo	7¼in	54
Imperiale	7¼in	54
Robusto Suprema	7¼in	54
Corona Inmensa	7¼in	47
Double Corona	7in	49
Cedar	7in	43
Flor de Llaneza	6½in	54
Flor de LaVonda	6½in	52
Plantation	6½in	30
Choix Supreme	6⅛in	49
Montecarlo	6⅛in	48
Robusto Larga	6in	54
Classic Corona	5⅝	45
Originale	5⅝in	45
Corona	5⅝in	45
Rectangulare	5⅝in	45
Habana Club	5½in	42
Tino	5½in	38
Elegante	5⅜in	29
Robusto	5in	54
Robusto Zavalla	5in	54
Rothschilde	5in	50
Reynita	5in	38
Petit Lonsdale	4⅝in	43
Cafe au Lait	4½in	35

Corona/5⅝in/Ring Gauge 45

EXCALIBUR

(Hoyo de Monterrey)

Ctry of Manu	Honduras
Filler	Dominican Republic/ Honduras/Nicaragua
Binder	Honduras
Wrapper	Connecticut
Flavor	Full
Quality	Excellent
Comment	Nutty and earthy tobacco flavors with typical Honduran spice

Vitolas

Name	Length	Ring Gauge
No.I	7¼in	54
Banquets	6¾in	48
No.II	6¾in	47
No.V	6¼in	45
No.III	6⅛in	48
No.IV	5⅝in	46
No.VI	5½in	38
No.VII	5in	43
Miniatures	3in	22

No.IV/5⅝in/Ring Gauge 46

EXCELSIOR

Ctry of Manu	Mexico
Filler	Mexico and Jamaica
Binder	Dominican Republic
Wrapper	Connecticut
Flavor	Mild to medium
Quality	Excellent
Comment	Excellent construction and draw framing a delicate smoke with a noticeable cedar edge to it

Vitolas

Name	Length	Ring Gauge
Individuale	8½in	52
No.5	8in	50
No.4	7in	48
No.2	6¾in	44
No.1	6¼in	42
No.3	5½in	52

Individuale/8½in/Ring Gauge 52

FELIPE GREGORIO

Ctry of Manu	Honduras
Filler	Honduras
Binder	Honduras
Wrapper	Honduras
Flavor	Medium
Quality	Good
Comment	Pleasant, smooth tobacco flavors but a very short aftertaste

Vitolas

Name	Length	Ring Gauge
Glorioso	7¾in	50
Suntuoso	7in	48
Belicoso	6in	Torpedo
Sereno	5¾in	42
Robusto	5in	52
Nino	4¼in	44

Robusto/5in/Ring Gauge 52

FONSECA

Ctry of Manu	Dominican Republic
Filler	Dominican Republic
Binder	Mexico
Wrapper	Connecticut
Flavor	Mild to medium
Quality	Good
Comment	A good burn and draw frame a smoke with a slightly grassy character

Vitolas

Name	Length	Ring Gauge
10-10	7in	50
7-9-9	6½in	46
8-9-9	6in	43
Triangular	5½in	56
5-50	5in	50
2-2	4¼in	40

7-9-9/6½in/Ring Gauge 46

FONSECA

Ctry of Manu	Cuba
Filler	Cuba
Binder	Cuba
Wrapper	Cuba
Flavor	Medium to full
Quality	Good
Comment	Strong, but lacking refinement, with leafy flavors

VITOLAS

Name	Length	Ring Gauge
No.1	6$\frac{3}{8}$in	44
Cosacos	5$\frac{1}{4}$in	40
Invictos	5$\frac{1}{4}$in	45
Delicias	4$\frac{7}{8}$in	40
K.D.T. Cadetes	4$\frac{1}{2}$in	36

K.D.T. CADETES/4$\frac{1}{2}$IN/RING GAUGE 36

GISPERT

Ctry of Manu	Cuba
Filler	Cuba
Binder	Cuba
Wrapper	Cuba
Flavor	Medium
Quality	Good
Comment	Starting off slightly bland but improving in the course of smoking to finish pleasant if modest

VITOLAS

Name	Length	Ring Gauge
Corona	5$\frac{5}{8}$in	42
Petit Corona de Luxe	5in	42
Habaneras No.2	4$\frac{5}{8}$in	35

CORONA/5$\frac{5}{8}$IN/RING GAUGE 42

GRIFFIN'S

Ctry of Manu	Dominican Republic
Filler	Dominican Republic
Binder	Dominican Republic
Wrapper	Connecticut
Flavor	Medium
Quality	Good
Comment	A pleasant start with flavors of mint and a hint of alcohol. However, it deteriorates in the second half

VITOLAS

Name	Length	Ring Gauge
Prestige	7$\frac{1}{2}$in	50
No.100	7in	38
No.200	7in	43
No.300	6$\frac{1}{4}$in	43
No.400	6in	38
No.500	5$\frac{1}{16}$in	43
Robusto	5in	50
Privilege	5in	32

ROBUSTO/5IN/RING GAUGE 50

HABANA GOLD

CTRY OF MANU	HONDURAS
FILLER	NICARAGUA
BINDER	NICARAGUA
WRAPPER	ECUADOR
FLAVOR	MILD TO MEDIUM
QUALITY	OUTSTANDING
COMMENT	A DELICIOUS SMOKE OF SOFT TOBACCO WITH A SWEET FLORAL CHARACTER AND FRUIT IN THE AFTERTASTE

VITOLAS

NAME	LENGTH	RING GAUGE
Presidente	8½in	52
Double Corona	7½in	46
Churchill	7in	52
No.2	6⅛in	52
Torpedo	6in	52
Corona	6in	44
Robusto	5in	50
Petite Corona	5in	42

CHURCHILL/7IN/RING GAUGE 52

HABANICA

CTRY OF MANU	NICARAGUA
FILLER	NICARAGUA
BINDER	NICARAGUA
WRAPPER	NICARAGUA
FLAVOR	MILD TO MEDIUM
QUALITY	EXCELLENT
COMMENT	AN UNSIGHTLY WRAPPER DID NOT BELONG TO THIS DELIGHTFUL SMOKE. SOFT AND GENTLE WITH A SWEET ASPECT, AND ENGAGING TO THE END

VITOLAS

NAME	LENGTH	RING GAUGE
Serie 747	7in	47
Serie 646	6in	46
Serie 638	6in	38
Serie 546	5¼in	46
Serie 550	5in	50

SERIE 550/5IN/RING GAUGE 50

HENRY CLAY

CTRY OF MANU	DOMINICAN REPUBLIC
FILLER	DOMINICAN REPUBLIC/BRAZIL/ INDONESIA
BINDER	DOMINICAN REPUBLIC/BRAZIL/ INDONESIA
WRAPPER	CONNECTICUT
FLAVOR	MILD TO MEDIUM
QUALITY	GOOD
COMMENT	STRAIGHTFORWARD BUT WELL-BALANCED TOBACCO FLAVORS

VITOLAS

NAME	LENGTH	RING GAUGE
Brevas Finas	6½in	48
No.7 Brevas Conservas	5⅝in	46
No.7 Brevas	5½in	42

BREVAS FINAS/6½IN/RING GAUGE 48

HOYO DE MONTERREY

CTRY OF MANU	CUBA
FILLER	CUBA
BINDER	CUBA
WRAPPER	CUBA
FLAVOR	MEDIUM TO FULL
QUALITY	OUTSTANDING
COMMENT	A GREAT WEALTH OF COMPLEX FLAVOR, CONSTRUCTED WITH ELEGANCE AND REFINEMENT

VITOLAS

NAME	LENGTH	RING GAUGE
Double Coronas	7⅝in	49
Epicures No.1	5⅝in	46
Coronas	5½in	42
Epicures No.2	4⅞in	50
Margaritas	4¾in	26
LE HOYO SERIES		
Du Gourmet	6⅝in	33
Des Dieux	6in	42
Du Dauphin	6in	38
Du Roi	5½in	42
Du Prince	5in	40
Du Depute	4¼in	38
Du Maire	3⅞in	30

CORONAS/5½IN/RING GAUGE 42

CUBAN HOYO DE MONTERREY CIGARS

HOYO DE MONTERREY

CTRY OF MANU	HONDURAS
FILLER	HONDURAS/NICARAGUA/ DOMINICAN REPUBLIC
BINDER	HONDURAS
WRAPPER	ECUADOR
FLAVOR	MEDIUM TO FULL
QUALITY	EXCELLENT
COMMENT	AN EARTHY AND ESPRESSO-STYLE SMOKE

VITOLAS

NAME	LENGTH	RING GAUGE
Presidents	8½in	52
Sultans	7¼in	54
Cuban Largos	7¼in	47
Largo Elegantes	7¼in	34
Cetros	7in	43
Double Corona	6¾in	48
No.1	6½in	43
Churchills	6¼in	45
Ambassadors	6¼in	44
Delights	6¼in	37
Governors	6⅛in	50
Culebras	6in	35
Coronas	5⅝in	46
Cafe Royales	5⅝in	43
Dreams	5¾in	46
Petit	5¾in	31
Super Hoyos	5½in	44
No.55	5¼in	43
Margaritas	5¼in	29
Sabrosos	5in	40
Rothschild	4½in	50
Demitasse	4in	39

ROTHSCHILD/4½IN/RING GAUGE 50

H UPMANN

CTRY OF MANU	DOMINICAN REPUBLIC
FILLER	DOMINICAN REPUBLIC/BRAZIL
BINDER	DOMINICAN REPUBLIC
WRAPPER	INDONESIAN
FLAVOR	MILD TO MEDIUM
QUALITY	EXCELLENT
COMMENT	A RESPECTABLE BALANCE OF TOBACCO FLAVORS IN A SOFT STYLE

VITOLAS

NAME	LENGTH	RING GAUGE
Corona Imperiales	7in	46
Monarch Tubes	7in	46
No.2000	7in	42
El Prado	7in	36
Extra Finos Gold Tube	6¾in	38
Panetela Cristal	6¾in	38
Director Royales	6⅝in	42
Lonsdales	6⅝in	42
Coronas Bravas	6½in	48
Finos Gold Tube	6⅛in	36
Naturales Tubes	6⅛in	36
Churchills	5⅝in	46
Coronas	5 9/16in	42
Corona Cristals	5 9/16in	42
Topacios	5¼in	43
Corona Major Tubes	5 5/16in	42
Petit Coronas	5 5/16in	42
Tubos Gold Tube	5 5/16in	42
Pequenos No.100	4½in	50
Pequenos No.200	4½in	42
Pequenos No.300	4½in	42
Demi Tasse	4½in	33
Aperitifs	4in	28
CABINET SELECTION		
Colombo	8in	50
Corsario	5½in	50
Robusto	4¾in	50

PETIT CORONAS/5 5/16IN/RING GAUGE 42

H UPMANN

CTRY OF MANU	CUBA
FILLER	CUBA
BINDER	CUBA
WRAPPER	CUBA
FLAVOR	MILD
QUALITY	OUTSTANDING
COMMENT	SOFT AND PERFECTLY BALANCED WITH HINTS OF ALL SORTS OF DELIGHTFUL FLAVORS

VITOLAS

NAME	LENGTH	RING GAUGE
Monarchs	7in	47
Monarcas	7in	47
Lonsdale	6½in	42
Upmann No.2	6⅛in	52
Grand Coronas	5¾in	40
Royal Coronas	5½in	42
Coronas	5½in	42
Coronas Majors	5⅛in	42
Petit Coronas	5in	42
Coronas Minors	4⅝in	40
Coronas Juniors	4½in	36
Petit Upmann	4½in	36
CABINET SELECTION		
Magnum	5½in	46
Connoisseurs No.1	5in	48

MONARCAS/7IN/RING GAUGE 47

JOSE BENITO

CTRY OF MANU	DOMINICAN REPUBLIC
FILLER	DOMINICAN REPUBLIC
BINDER	HONDURAS/NICARAGUA
WRAPPER	INDONESIAN
FLAVOR	MILD TO MEDIUM
QUALITY	POOR
COMMENT	BLUNT AND GRITTY TOBACCO FLAVORS THAT LACK BALANCE

VITOLAS

NAME	LENGTH	RING GAUGE
Magnum	8¾in	60
Presidente	7¾in	50
Churchill	7in	50
Corona	6¾in	43
Panatela	6¾in	38
Palma	6in	43
Petite	5½in	38
Havanitos	5in	25
Rothschild	4¾in	50
Chico	4¼in	32

CHURCHILL/7IN/RING GAUGE 50

JOSE MARTI

CTRY OF MANU	DOMINICAN REPUBLIC
FILLER	DOMINICAN REPUBLIC
BINDER	DOMINICAN REPUBLIC
WRAPPER	CONNECTICUT
FLAVOR	MILD TO MEDIUM
QUALITY	AVERAGE
COMMENT	A STINGY DRAW INTERFERED WITH THE FLAVOR OF THIS CIGAR WHICH CAME ACROSS AS GRASSY AND A BIT SHALLOW

VITOLAS

NAME	LENGTH	RING GAUGE
Marti	7½in	50
Palma	7in	42
Macea	6⅞in	44
Creme	6in	34
Robusto	5½in	50
Corona	5½in	40

MARTI/7½IN/RING GAUGE 50

JOYA DE NICARAGUA

CTRY OF MANU	NICARAGUA
FILLER	NICARAGUA
BINDER	NICARAGUA
WRAPPER	ECUADOR
FLAVOR	MILD TO MEDIUM
QUALITY	EXCELLENT
COMMENT	A CHARMING SMOKE WITH SWEET SPICES AND HINTS OF AROMATIC WOODS

VITOLAS

NAME	LENGTH	RING GAUGE
Viajante	8½in	52
Churchill	6⅞in	49
No.5	6⅞in	35
No.1	6⅝in	44
No.6	6in	52
Petit	5½in	38
Consul	4½in	51
MADURO		
Presidente	7½in	50
Toro	6in	50
Robusto	4¾in	52

CHURCHILL/6⅞IN/RING GAUGE 49

J.R. SPECIAL JAMAICAN

CTRY OF MANU	DOMINICAN REPUBLIC
FILLER	DOMINICAN REPUBLIC
BINDER	MEXICO
WRAPPER	CONNECTICUT
FLAVOR	MILD
QUALITY	EXCELLENT
COMMENT	A SOFT CHARACTER WITH CREAMY COFFEE FLAVORS

VITOLAS

NAME	LENGTH	RING GAUGE
Rey del Rey	9in	60
Mayfair	7in	60
Pyramid	7in	52
Nobles	7in	50
Churchill	7in	50
Size A	6½in	44
Fancytale Shape	6½in	43
Bonita Obsequio	6in	50
Size D	6in	50
Size B	6in	44
Size C	5½in	44
Pica	5in	32

SIZE D/6IN/RING GAUGE 50

SPECIAL JAMAICAN CIGARS

J.R. ULTIMATE

CTRY OF MANU	HONDURAS
FILLER	HONDURAS
BINDER	HONDURAS
WRAPPER	HONDURAS
FLAVOR	MEDIUM
QUALITY	GOOD
COMMENT	STARTING OFF PLAIN WITH A PARSIMONIOUS DRAW, THE CIGAR DEVELOPED VERY WELL, ENDING RICH AND SATISFYING

VITOLAS

NAME	LENGTH	RING GAUGE
Estelo	8½in	52
President	8½in	52
No.10	8¼in	47
Super Cetro	8¼in	43
No.1	7¼in	54
Cetro	7in	42
Palma Extra	6⅞in	38
Slims	6⅞in	36
Double Corona	6¾in	48
No.5	6⅛in	44
Padron	6in	54
Toro	6in	50
Corona	5⅝in	45
Petit Cetro	5½in	38
Corona Tubo	5⅜in	45
Habenella	5in	28
Petit Corona	4⅝in	43
Rothschild	4½in	50

NO.1/7¼IN/RING GAUGE 54

JUAN CLEMENTE

CTRY OF MANU	DOMINICAN REPUBLIC
FILLER	DOMINICAN REPUBLIC
BINDER	DOMINICAN REPUBLIC
WRAPPER	CONNECTICUT
FLAVOR	MILD
QUALITY	POOR
COMMENT	A POORLY CONSTRUCTED CIGAR WHOSE APPEARANCE DOES NOTHING TO MAKE UP FOR ITS BLAND FLAVORS

VITOLAS

NAME	LENGTH	RING GAUGE
Gargantua	13in	50
Gigante	9in	50
Especiales	7 1/2in	38
Churchills	6 7/8in	46
Panatelas	6 1/2in	34
Grand Coronas	6in	42
Especiales No.2	5 7/8in	38
Coronas	5in	42
530	5in	30
Rothschilds	4 7/8in	50
Mini-Cigar	4 1/16in	22
Demi-Coronas	4in	40
Demi-Tasse	3 10/16in	34
CLUB SELECTION 500 ANNIVERSARIO		
No.3	7in	44
No.5 Obeliscos	6in	52
No.1	6in	50
No.4	5 3/4in	42
No.2	4 1/2in	46

ESPECIALES 7 1/2IN/RING GAUGE 38

JUAN CLEMENTE CIGARS

JUAN LOPEZ

CTRY OF MANU	CUBA
FILLER	CUBA
BINDER	CUBA
WRAPPER	CUBA
FLAVOR	MILD
QUALITY	GOOD
COMMENT	A STRAIGHTFORWARD AND PLEASANT BLEND OF TOBACCO FLAVORS

VITOLAS

NAME	LENGTH	RING GAUGE
Coronas	5 5/8in	42
Petit Coronas	5in	42
Placeras	5in	34
Slimaranas	4 3/4in	32
Patricias	4 1/2in	40

SLIMARANAS/4 3/4IN/RING GAUGE 32

LA AURORA

CTRY OF MANU	DOMINICAN REPUBLIC
FILLER	DOMINICAN REPUBLIC
BINDER	DOMINICAN REPUBLIC
WRAPPER	CAMEROON
FLAVOR	MEDIUM
QUALITY	GOOD
COMMENT	A PLEASANT SMOKE WITH A HINT OF MINT

VITOLAS

NAME	LENGTH	RING GAUGE
Palmas Extras	6¾in	35
Bristol Especiales	6⅜in	48
Cetros	6⅜in	35
Aurora No.4	5¼in	42
Sublimes	5in	38
Coronas	5in	35

AURORA NO.4/5¼IN/RING GAUGE 42

LA CORONA

CTRY OF MANU	DOMINICAN REPUBLIC
FILLER	DOMINICAN REPUBLIC
BINDER	DOMINICAN REPUBLIC
WRAPPER	CONNECTICUT
FLAVOR	MILD TO MEDIUM
QUALITY	GOOD
COMMENT	SMOOTH, EARTHY, AND SAVORY IN FLAVOR

VITOLAS

NAME	LENGTH	RING GAUGE
Directors	6½in	46
Aristocrats	6⅛in	36
Long Corona	6in	43
Corona Chicas	5½in	42

CORONA CHICA/5½IN/RING GAUGE 42

LA CORONA CIGARS

LA DIVA

CTRY OF MANU	DOMINICAN REPUBLIC
FILLER	DOMINICAN REPUBLIC
BINDER	DOMINICAN REPUBLIC
WRAPPER	CONNECTICUT
FLAVOR	MILD TO MEDIUM
QUALITY	GOOD
COMMENT	THE FIRST HALF IS DOMINATED BY A PLEASANT SWEET TOBACCO STYLE WHICH DWINDLES AWAY TOO SOON

VITOLAS

NAME	LENGTH	RING GAUGE
Churchill	8in	50
Torpedo	7in	54
Corona	6in	44
Figurado	5½in	48
Robusto	4½in	50

TORPEDO/7IN/RING GAUGE 54

LA FINCA

CTRY OF MANU	NICARAGUA
FILLER	NICARAGUA
BINDER	NICARAGUA
WRAPPER	NICARAGUA
FLAVOR	MILD TO MEDIUM
QUALITY	GOOD
COMMENT	FAIRLY STRAIGHTFORWARD TOBACCO FLAVOR APART FROM FAINT AND PLEASING HINTS OF COCOA AND COFFEE

VITOLAS

NAME	LENGTH	RING GAUGE
Gran Finca	8½in	52
Bolivar	7½in	50
Flora	7in	36
Romeo	6½in	42
Joya	6in	50
Pico	6in	36
Corona	5½in	42
Robusto	4½in	50
Petit Corona	4½in	42

BOLIVAR/7½IN/RING GAUGE 50

LA GLORIA CUBANA

CTRY OF MANU	CUBA
FILLER	CUBA
BINDER	CUBA
WRAPPER	CUBA
FLAVOR	MEDIUM TO FULL
QUALITY	EXCELLENT
COMMENT	A RICH, SPICY, AND AROMATIC SMOKE

VITOLAS

NAME	LENGTH	RING GAUGE
Medaille D'Or 1	$7\frac{5}{16}$in	36
Tainos	7in	47
Medaille D'Or 3	6⅞in	28
Medaille D'Or 2	$6\frac{11}{16}$in	43
Cetros	6½in	42
Sabrosas	6⅛in	42
Medaille D'Or 4	6in	32
Tapados	$5\frac{5}{16}$in	42
Minutos	4½in	40

SABROSAS/6⅛IN/RING GAUGE 42

LA INVICTA

CTRY OF MANU	HONDURAS
FILLER	HONDURAS
BINDER	HONDURAS
WRAPPER	HONDURAS
FLAVOR	MEDIUM TO FULL
QUALITY	GOOD
COMMENT	SPICY AND A BIT SWEET

VITOLAS

NAME	LENGTH	RING GAUGE
Especiales	6⅞in	36
Churchills	6¾in	47
Coronas Extra	6¼in	43
Coronas	5½in	42
Panetelas	5¼in	29
Petit Coronas	5in	42
Gordas	4½in	50

GORDAS/4½IN/RING GAUGE 50

LA INVICTA CIGARS

LA UNICA

CTRY OF MANU	DOMINICAN REPUBLIC
FILLER	DOMINICAN REPUBLIC
BINDER	DOMINICAN REPUBLIC
WRAPPER	CONNECTICUT
FLAVOR	MEDIUM
QUALITY	AVERAGE
COMMENT	A POOR DRAW INTERFERED WITH THE FLAVOR WHICH CAME ACROSS AS GRITTY TOBACCO

VITOLAS

NAME	LENGTH	RING GAUGE
No.100	8½in	52
No.200	7in	49
No.300	6¾in	44
No.400	4½in	50
No.50	5½in	42

NO.300/6¾IN/RING GAUGE 44

LAS CABRILLAS

CTRY OF MANU	HONDURAS
FILLER	ASSORTED
BINDER	ASSORTED
WRAPPER	ASSORTED
FLAVOR	MILD
QUALITY	GOOD
COMMENT	AFTER A SLOW START THIS CIGAR SETTLED DOWN TO A TOBACCO CHARACTER TOUCHED BY LIGHT AND FRESH MINTINESS

VITOLAS

NAME	LENGTH	RING GAUGE
Columbus	8¼in	52
Balboa	7½in	54
Maximilian	7in	56
DeSoto	6⅞in	50
Coronado	6⅞in	35
Ponce de Leon	6⅝in	44
Magellan	6in	42
Pizarro	5½in	32
Cortez	4¾in	50

BALBOA/7½IN/RING GAUGE 54

LEON JIMENES

CTRY OF MANU	DOMINICAN REPUBLIC
FILLER	DOMINICAN REPUBLIC
BINDER	DOMINICAN REPUBLIC
WRAPPER	CONNECTICUT
FLAVOR	MILD
QUALITY	GOOD
COMMENT	STRAIGHTFORWARD BLEND OF WELL-BALANCED TOBACCO FLAVORS

VITOLAS

NAME	LENGTH	RING GAUGE
No.1	7½in	50
No.2	7in	47
No.3	6½in	42
No.4	5⅝in	42
Robusto	5½in	50
No.5	5in	38

ROBUSTO/5½IN/RING GAUGE 50

LICENCIADOS

CTRY OF MANU	DOMINICAN REPUBLIC
FILLER	DOMINICAN REPUBLIC
BINDER	DOMINICAN REPUBLIC
WRAPPER	CONNECTICUT
FLAVOR	MILD
QUALITY	EXCELLENT
COMMENT	AFTER A MODEST START THIS CIGAR DEVELOPED NICELY TO SMOOTH AND CREAMY FLAVORS DESPITE SOME CONSTRUCTION PROBLEMS

VITOLAS

NAME	LENGTH	RING GAUGE
Soberano	8½in	52
Presidente	8in	50
Churchill	7in	50
Panetela	7in	38
Excelente	6¾in	43
Toro	6in	50
Licenciados No.4	5¾in	43
Wavell	5in	50

PANETELA 7IN/RING GAUGE 38

MACANUDO

Ctry of Manu	Dominican Republic/Jamaica
Filler	Dominican Republic Jamaica/Mexico
Binder	Mexico
Wrapper	Connecticut
Flavor	Mild
Quality	Outstanding
Comment	An excellent draw and burn frame a cigar with a delicious milk coffee character and a sweet undertone

Macanudo cigars with various bands

Vitolas

Name	Length	Ring Gauge
Duke of Wellington	8½in	38
Prince Philip	7½in	49
Vintage No.1	7½in	49
Sovereign	7in	45
Somerset	7in	34
Portofino	7in	34
Earl of Lonsdale	6¾in	38
Vintage No.II	6 9/16in	43
Baron de Rothschild	6½in	42
Amatista	6¼in	42
Claybourne	6in	31
Hampton Court	5¾in	43
Vintage No.III	5 9/16in	43
Hyde Park	5½in	49
Duke of Devon	5½in	42
Lord Claridge	5½in	38
Quill	5¼in	28
Petit Corona	5in	38
Vintage No.IV	4½in	47
Ascot	4 3/16in	32
Caviar	4in	36

Hampton Court/5¾in/Ring Gauge 43

MATACAN

Ctry of Manu	Mexico
Filler	Mexico
Binder	Mexico
Wrapper	Mexico
Flavor	Medium
Quality	Good
Comment	A curious tobacco flavor that is not unpleasant

Vitolas

Name	Length	Ring Gauge
No.8	8in	52
No.1	7½in	50
No.10	6⅞in	54
No.3	6⅝in	46
No.4	6⅝in	42
No.6	6⅝in	35
No.2	6in	50
No.5	6in	42
No.9	5in	32
No.7	4¾in	50

No.5/6in/Ring Gauge 42

Matacan cigars

MOCHA

CTRY OF MANU	HONDURAS
FILLER	HONDURAS
BINDER	HONDURAS
WRAPPER	HONDURAS
FLAVOR	MEDIUM TO FULL
QUALITY	AVERAGE
COMMENT	A WOODY AND NUTTY CHARACTER BUT WITH A SLIGHTLY ROUGH EDGE

VITOLAS

NAME	LENGTH	RING GAUGE
Rembrandt	8½in	52
Patroon	7½in	50
Lord	6½in	42
Allegro	6½in	36
Renaissance	6in	50
Sovereign	5½in	42
Baron Rothchild	4½in	52
Petite	4½in	42

LORD/6½IN/RIING GAUGE 42

MONTECRISTO

CTRY OF MANU	CUBA
FILLER	CUBA
BINDER	CUBA
WRAPPER	CUBA
FLAVOR	MEDIUM TO FULL
QUALITY	OUTSTANDING
COMMENT	CHARMING AND INTRIGUING, WITH OPULENT FLAVORS OF ROAST NUTS AND TOBACCO, AND A SLIGHT TANGY EDGE

VITOLAS

NAME	LENGTH	RING GAUGE
Montecristo "A"	9¼in	47
Especial	7½in	38
No.1	6½in	42
No.2	6⅛in	52
Tubos	6in	42
Especial No.2	6in	38
No.3	5½in	42
Petit Tubos	5in	42
No.4	5in	42
Joyitas	4½in	26
No.5	4in	40

NO.2/6⅛IN/RING GAUGE 52

ESPECIAL NO.2/6IN/RING GAUGE 38

CUBAN MONTECRISTO CIGAR BOX

MONTECRUZ

Ctry of Manu	Dominican Republic
Filler	Dominican Republic/Brazil
Binder	Dominican Republic
Wrapper	Cameroon
Flavor	Mild to medium
Quality	Excellent
Comment	Well-balanced tobacco flavors with a soft and lasting aftertaste

Montecruz cigars

Vitolas

Name	Length	Ring Gauge
Individuals	8in	46
No.200	7¼in	46
No.205	7in	42
No.255	7in	36
No.280	7in	28
Collusus	6½in	50
No.210	6½in	42
No.250	6½in	38
No.201	6¼in	46
Tubulares	6⅛in	36
Tubos	6in	42
No.276	6in	32
No.281	6in	28
Seniors	5¾in	35
No.265	5½in	38
No.220	5½in	42
Juniors	5¼in	33
Cedar Aged	5in	42
No.230	5in	42
No.282	5in	28
No.270	4¾in	36
Robusto	4½in	49
Chicos	4in	28

No.210/6½in/Ring Gauge 42

MONTESINO

Ctry of Manu	Dominican Republic
Filler	Dominican Republic
Binder	Dominican Republic
Wrapper	Dominican Republic
Flavor	Mild
Quality	Good
Comment	A straightforward tobacco character that comes from a good burn and draw

Vitolas

Name	Length	Ring Gauge
Napoleon Grande	7in	46
No.1	6⅞in	43
Gran Corona	6¾in	48
Fumas	6¾in	44
No.3	6¾in	36
No.2	6¼in	44
Diplomatico	5½in	42

No.1/6⅞in/Ring Gauge 43

Montesino cigars

NAT SHERMAN

CTRY OF MANU	DOMINICAN REPUBLIC
FILLER	DOMINICAN REPUBLIC
BINDER	DOMINICAN REPUBLIC
WRAPPER	CONNECTICUT
FLAVOR	MILD
QUALITY	GOOD
COMMENT	A FIRST IMPRESSION OF CHUNKY TOBACCO FLAVORS QUICKLY MAKES WAY FOR A PLEASANT AND BALANCED BLEND

VITOLAS

NAME	LENGTH	RING GAUGE
Manhattan selection*		
Gramercy	$6\frac{3}{4}$in	43
Chelsea	$6\frac{1}{2}$in	38
Tribeca	6in	31
Sutton	$5\frac{1}{2}$in	49
Beekman	$5\frac{1}{4}$in	28

*Other lines include the Gotham, City Desk, Landmark, and Exchange selections.

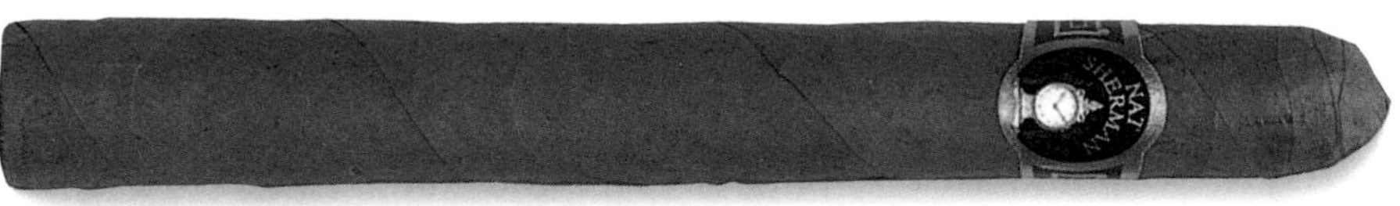

CHELSEA/$6\frac{1}{2}$IN/RING GAUGE 38

OSCAR

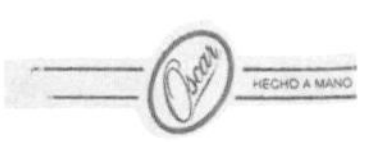

CTRY OF MANU	DOMINICAN REPUBLIC
FILLER	DOMINICAN REPUBLIC
BINDER	DOMINICAN REPUBLIC
WRAPPER	CONNECTICUT
FLAVOR	MILD
QUALITY	GOOD
COMMENT	A VERY ENJOYABLE FRAGRANT AND LIGHT FIRST HALF WAS MARRED BY A PREMATURE SHARPNESS CREEPING IN THE SECOND

VITOLAS

NAME	LENGTH	RING GAUGE
Don Oscar	9in	46
Supreme	8in	48
No.700	7in	54
No.200	7in	44
No.100	7in	38
No.300	$6\frac{1}{4}$in	44
No.400	6in	38
No.500	$5\frac{1}{2}$in	50
Prince	5in	30
No.600	$4\frac{1}{2}$in	50
No.800	4in	42
Oscarito	4in	20

NO.300/$6\frac{1}{4}$IN/RING GAUGE 44

PADRON

CTRY OF MANU	NICARAGUA/HONDURAS
FILLER	NICARAGUA
BINDER	NICARAGUA
WRAPPER	NICARAGUA
FLAVOR	MILD TO MEDIUM
QUALITY	GOOD
COMMENT	AN EXTREMELY WELL-MADE CIGAR WITH A DISTINCTIVE TASTE THAT WAS UNCONVENTIONAL FOR A CIGAR

VITOLAS

NAME	LENGTH	RING GAUGE
Magnum	9in	50
Grand Reserve	8in	41
Executive	$7\frac{1}{2}$in	50
Churchill	$6\frac{7}{8}$in	46
Ambassador	$6\frac{7}{8}$in	42
Panetela	$6\frac{7}{8}$in	36
Palmas	$6\frac{5}{16}$in	42
3000	$5\frac{1}{2}$in	52
Londres	$5\frac{1}{2}$in	42
Chicos	$5\frac{1}{2}$in	36
2000	5in	50
Delicias	$4\frac{7}{8}$in	46

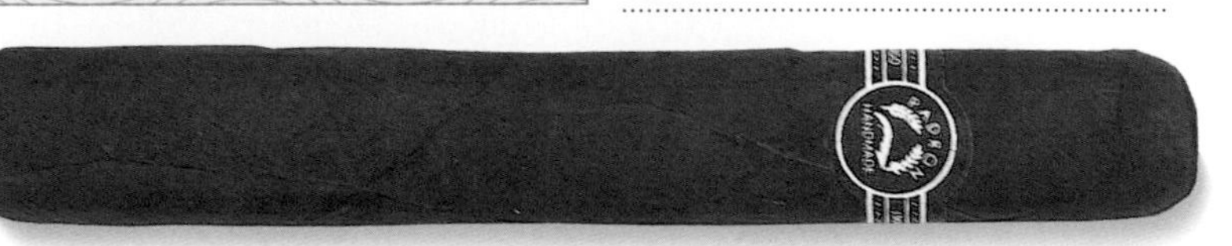

3000/$5\frac{1}{2}$IN/RING GAUGE 52

PADRON ANIVERSARIO

CTRY OF MANU	NICARAGUA/HONDURAS
FILLER	NICARAGUA
BINDER	NICARAGUA
WRAPPER	NICARAGUA
FLAVOR	MEDIUM
QUALITY	EXCELLENT
COMMENT	AN EARTHY CIGAR, SMOOTH, AND WITH NO SHARP EDGES

VITOLAS

NAME	LENGTH	RING GAUGE
Diplomatico	7in	50
Pyramid	6⅞in	52
Monarca	6½in	46
Superior	6½in	42
Corona	6in	42
Exclusivo	5½in	50

EXCLUSIVO/5½IN/RING GAUGE 50

PARTAGAS

CTRY OF MANU	DOMINICAN REPUBLIC
FILLER	DOMINICAN REPUBLIC/MEXICO
BINDER	MEXICO
WRAPPER	CAMEROON
FLAVOR	MEDIUM TO FULL
QUALITY	EXCELLENT
COMMENT	WELL-MADE WITH A LOVELY NUTTY AND SPICY CHARACTER

VITOLAS

NAME	LENGTH	RING GAUGE
No.10	7½in	49
Tubos	7in	34
8-9-8	6⅞in	44
No.1	6¾in	43
Humitube	6¾in	43
Maduro	6¼in	48
Almirantes	6¼in	47
No.6	6in	34
Sabroso	5⅞in	44
No.2	5¾in	43
Naturales	5½in	50
No.3	5¼in	43
No.5	5¼in	28
No.4	5in	38
Robusto	4½in	49
Puritos	4⅞in	32

NO.3/5¼IN/RING GAUGE 43

DOMINICAN REPUBLIC PARTAGAS CIGARS

PARTAGAS

Ctry of Manu	Cuba
Filler	Cuba
Binder	Cuba
Wrapper	Cuba
Flavor	Full
Quality	Outstanding
Comment	A delightful variety of generous earthy and spicy flavors, delivered by an ample and cool draw

Cuban Partagas cigar box

Vitolas

Name	Length	Ring Gauge
Lusitanias	7⅝in	49
Churchill De Luxe	7in	47
Palmes Grandes	7in	33
Partagas de Partagas No.1	6¾in	43
Seleccion Privada No.1	6¾in	43
8-9-8	6¾in	43
Lonsdale	6½in	42
Corona Grande	6in	42
Culebras (twisted)	5$^{11}/_{16}$in	39
Corona	5½in	42
Charlotte	5½in	35
Petit Corona	5in	42
Series D No.4	4⅞in	50
Très Petit Corona	4½in	40
Shorts	4$^{5}/_{16}$in	42

8-9-8/6¾in/Ring Gauge 43

PAUL GARMIRIAN

Ctry of Manu	Dominican Republic
Filler	Dominican Republic
Binder	Dominican Republic
Wrapper	Connecticut
Flavor	Medium
Quality	Good
Comment	A well-fashioned cigar with predominantly green and grassy flavors

Paul Garmirian cigars

Vitolas

Name	Length	Ring Gauge
Celebration	9in	50
Double Corona	7⅝in	50
No.1	7½in	38
Churchill	7in	48
Belicoso	6½in	52
Corona Grande	6½in	46
Lonsdale	6½in	42
Connoisseur	6in	50
Especial	5¾in	38
Belicoso Fino	5½in	52
Epicure	5½in	50
Corona	5½in	42
Robusto	5in	50
Petit Corona	5in	43
No.2	4¾in	48
Petit Bouquet	4½in	38
No.5	4in	40
Bombones	3½in	43

Corona/5½in/Ring Gauge 42

PETERSON

Ctry of Manu	Dominican Republic
Filler	Dominican Republic
Binder	Dominican Republic
Wrapper	Connecticut
Flavor	Mild to medium
Quality	Good
Comment	Spicy tobacco flavor with an undercurrent of cedar

Vitolas

Name	Length	Ring Gauge
Presidente	7½in	50
Churchill	7in	48
Toro	6in	50
Corona	5¾in	43
Petit Corona	5in	43
Robusto	4¾in	50
Tres Petit Corona	4½in	38

Robusto/4¾in/Ring Gauge 50

PETRUS

Ctry of Manu	Honduras
Filler	Honduras
Binder	Honduras
Wrapper	Ecuador
Flavor	Mild
Quality	Excellent
Comment	Good-looking and well-made with a soft and slightly sweet character

Vitolas

Name	Length	Ring Gauge
Lord Byron	8in	38
Double Corona	7¾in	50
Churchill	7in	50
No.2	6¼in	44
No.3	6in	50
Palma Fina	6in	38
No.4	5⅝in	38
Corona Sublime	5½in	46
Antonius	5in	Torpedo
Gregorius	5in	42
Rothschild	4¾in	50
Chantaco	4¾in	35
Duchess	4½in	30

Rothschild/4¾in/Ring Gauge 50

PLEIADES

Ctry of Manu	Dominican Republic
Filler	Dominican Republic
Binder	Dominican Republic
Wrapper	Connecticut
Flavor	Mild to medium
Quality	Good
Comment	Fresh, floral, and slightly piquant

Vitolas

Name	Length	Ring Gauge
Aldebran	8½in	50
Saturne	8in	46
Neptune	7½in	42
Sirius	6⅞in	46
Uranus	6⅞in	34
Orion	5¾in	42
Antares	5½in	40
Venus	5⅛in	28
Pluton	5in	50
Perseus	5in	34
Mars	5in	28

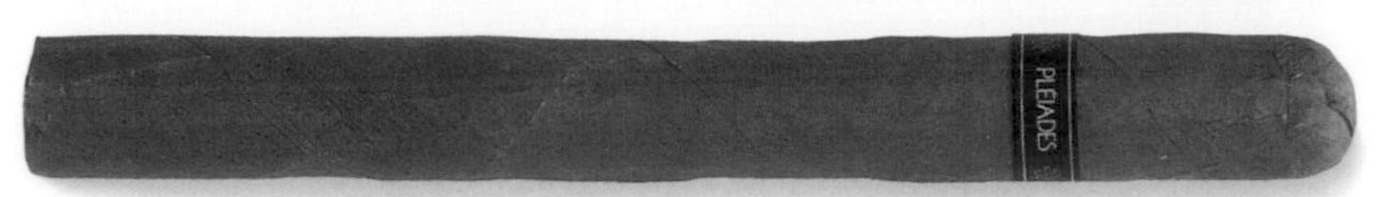

Orion/5¾in/Ring Gauge 42

POR LARRANAGA

CTRY OF MANU	CUBA
FILLER	CUBA
BINDER	CUBA
WRAPPER	CUBA
FLAVOR	MEDIUM TO FULL
QUALITY	GOOD
COMMENT	RICH AND AROMATIC, WITH PERSISTENT SWEETNESS

VITOLAS

NAME	LENGTH	RING GAUGE
Lonsdale	6½in	42
Corona	5½in	42
Petit Corona	5in	42
Small Corona	4½in	40

CORONA/5½IN/RING GAUGE 42

POR LARRANAGA

CTRY OF MANU	DOMINICAN REPUBLIC
FILLER	DOMINICAN REPUBLIC
BINDER	DOMINICAN REPUBLIC
WRAPPER	CONNECTICUT
FLAVOR	MEDIUM
QUALITY	GOOD
COMMENT	WELL-MADE AND ALIVE WITH FLAVOR

VITOLAS

NAME	LENGTH	RING GAUGE
Fabulosos	7in	50
Delicados	6½in	36
Cetros	6⅞in	42
Pyramids	6in	50
Nacionales	5 9/16in	42
Robusto	5in	50
Petit Cetros	5in	38

FABULOSO/7IN/RING GAUGE 50

ROBUSTO/5IN/RING GAUGE 50

DOMINICAN REPUBLIC POR LARRANAGA CIGARS

PRIMO DEL REY

Ctry of Manu	Dominican Republic
Filler	Dominican Republic/Mexico
Binder	Dominican Republic
Wrapper	Indonesia
Flavor	Medium
Quality	Excellent
Comment	Pleasant from the first puff with a thick tobacco and chocolate flavor

Vitolas

Name	Length	Ring Gauge
Aguilas	8in	52
Soberanos	7½in	50
Presidentes	$6\frac{13}{16}$in	44
Seleccion No.1	$6\frac{13}{16}$in	42
Seleccion No.3	$6\frac{13}{16}$in	36
Chavon	6½in	41
Churchill	6¼in	48
Seleccion No.2	6¼in	42
Reales	6⅛in	36
Cazadores	6⅙in	44
Almirantes	6in	50
Panetela Extras	$5\frac{15}{16}$in	34
Seleccion No.4	5½in	42
Panetelas	5⅜in	34
No.100	4½in	50
Cortos	4in	28
Club selection		
Barons	8½in	52
Regals	7in	50
Aristocrats	6¾in	48
Nobles	6¼in	44

Primo del Rey cigars

Chavon/6½in/Ring Gauge 41

PUNCH

Ctry of Manu	Cuba
Filler	Cuba
Binder	Cuba
Wrapper	Cuba
Flavor	Medium
Quality	Outstanding
Comment	Refined, well-balanced, and smooth tobacco flavors

Vitolas

Name	Length	Ring Gauge
Diademas Extra	9¼in	47
Double Coronas	7⅝in	49
Churchills	7in	47
Coronas	5⅝in	42
Punch – Punch	5½in	46
Royal Coronations	5½in	42
Coronations	5in	42
Petit Coronas	5in	42
Margaritas	4¾in	26
Petit Coronations	4½in	40
Coronets	4½in	40
Punchinellos	4½in	34
Tres Petit Coronas	4¼in	42
Petit Punch	4in	40

Petit Punch/4in/Ring Gauge 40

Punchinello/4½in/Ring Gauge 34

PUNCH

Ctry of Manu	Honduras
Filler	Honduras/Nicaragua/ Dominican Republic
Binder	Honduras
Wrapper	Ecuador
Flavor	Mild to medium
Quality	Excellent
Comment	Pleasant tobacco character with a bit of spiciness

Vitolas

Name	Length	Ring Gauge
Presidente	8½in	42
Chateau Lafitte	7¼in	52
Grand Diademas	7⅛in	52
Diademas	7⅛in	52
Elegante	7⅛in	36
Casa Grande	7in	46
Monarcas	6¾in	48
Double Corona	6⅝in	48
Chateau Corona	6½in	44
No.1	6½in	42
Bristol	6¼in	50
Britannia Delux	6¼in	50
Punch	6⅛in	43
Superiores Delux	5⅝in	46
Chateau Margaux	5½in	46
No.75	5½in	43
Superior	5in	50
Rothschild	4½in	48

Presidente/8½in/Ring Gauge 42

Honduran Punch cigars

RAFAEL GONZALEZ

Ctry of Manu	Cuba
Filler	Cuba
Binder	Cuba
Wrapper	Cuba
Flavor	Mild
Quality	Outstanding
Comment	Well-balanced and with an overall delicate but charming tobacco character

Vitolas

Name	Length	Ring Gauge
Slenderella	7in	28
Lonsdale	6½in	42
Corona Extra	5⅝in	46
Petit Corona	5in	42
Petit Lonsdale	5in	42
Panetela Extra	5in	37
Panetela	4⅝in	34
Très Petit Lonsdale	4½in	40
Cigarrito	4½in	26
Demi Tasse	4in	30

Petit Corona/5in/Ring Gauge 42

RAMON ALLONES

Ctry of Manu	Cuba
Filler	Cuba
Binder	Cuba
Wrapper	Cuba
Flavor	Full
Quality	Outstanding
Comment	Typical of the style of the Partagas factory where it is made this cigar is rich and complex, with powerful but elegant flavor

Vitolas

Name	Length	Ring Gauge
Gigantes	$7\frac{1}{2}$in	49
8-9-8	$6\frac{11}{16}$in	43
Coronas	$5\frac{5}{8}$in	42
Petit Coronas	5in	42
Panetela	5in	35
Specially Selected	$4\frac{13}{16}$in	50
Ramonitas	$4\frac{13}{16}$in	26
Small Club Coronas	$4\frac{3}{8}$in	42

Gigantes/$7\frac{1}{2}$in/Ring Gauge 49

Cuban Ramon Allones cigars

RAMON ALLONES

Ctry of Manu	Dominican Republic
Filler	Dominican Republic/ Jamaica/Mexico
Binder	Mexico
Wrapper	Cameroon
Flavor	Medium to full
Quality	Excellent
Comment	A rich black coffee flavor with an underlying sweetness

Vitolas

Name	Length	Ring Gauge
Redondos	7in	49
A	7in	45
Trumps	$6\frac{3}{4}$in	43
Crystals	$6\frac{3}{4}$in	43
B	$6\frac{1}{2}$in	42
D	5in	42

B/$6\frac{1}{2}$in/Ring Gauge 42

RIATA

CTRY OF MANU	HONDURAS
FILLER	HONDURAS
BINDER	HONDURAS
WRAPPER	HONDURAS
FLAVOR	MEDIUM
QUALITY	EXCELLENT
COMMENT	AMPLE IN SPICY AND EARTHY FLAVOR

VITOLAS

NAME	LENGTH	RING GAUGE
1000	8in	52
900	7½in	50
100	7in	30
600	6⅞in	48
200	6⅞in	35
500	6⅝in	44
800	6¼in	50
300	6in	42
It's a Boy	6in	42
It's a Girl	6in	42
400	5½in	44
700	4¾in	50

NO.1000/8IN/RING GAUGE 52

ROLANDO

CTRY OF MANU	DOMINICAN REPUBLIC
FILLER	DOMINICAN REPUBLIC
BINDER	DOMINICAN REPUBLIC
WRAPPER	CONNECTICUT
FLAVOR	MEDIUM
QUALITY	AVERAGE
COMMENT	NEUTRAL FLAVOR THAT DOES NOT DEVELOP MUCH

VITOLAS

NAME	LENGTH	RING GAUGE
Numero 2	7½in	48
Perfecto	7in	44
Pyramid	6½in	54
Numero 3	6in	50
Numero 4	6in	43
Robusto	4¾in	52

ROBUSTO/4¾IN/RING GAUGE 52

ROMEO Y JULIETA

CTRY OF MANU	CUBA
FILLER	CUBA
BINDER	CUBA
WRAPPER	CUBA
FLAVOR	MILD TO MEDIUM
QUALITY	OUTSTANDING
COMMENT	DELICIOUS AND COMPLEX TOBACCO AND COCOA FLAVORS THAT HAVE A GENTLE BUT FIRM NATURE AND A LONG AFTERTASTE

VITOLAS

NAME	LENGTH	RING GAUGE
Prince of Wales	7in	47
Churchills	7in	47
Shakespeares	6⅞in	28
Cedros No.1	6½in	42
Corona Grande	6in	42
Belicosos	5½in	52
Exhibition No.3	5½in	46
Coronas	5½in	42
Cedros No.2	5½in	42
Exhibition No.4	5in	48
Petit Coronas	5in	42
Cedros No.3	5in	42
Tres Petit Coronas	4½in	40
Petit Julietas	4in	30

EXHIBITION NO.4/5IN/RING GAUGE 48

ROMEO Y JULIETA

Ctry of Manu	Dominican Republic
Filler	Dominican Republic
Binder	Mexico
Wrapper	Connecticut
Flavor	Mild
Quality	Good
Comment	A light milky start that gives way to a leafy character

Dominican Republic Romeo Y Julieta cigars

Vitolas

Name	Length	Ring Gauge
Monarcas	8in	52
Churchills	7in	50
Presidentes	7in	43
Delgados	7in	32
Cetros	6½in	44
Romeos (torpedo)	6in	46
Indonesian		
Palmas	6in	43
Brevas	5⅝in	38
Coronas	5½in	44
Panatelas	5¼in	35
Rothschilds	5in	50
Chiquitas	4¼in	32
Vintage V	7½in	50
Vintage VI	7in	60
Vintage IV	7in	48
Vintage II	6in	46
Vintage I	6in	43
Vintage III	4½in	50

chiquita/4¼in/Ring Gauge 32

Corona/5½in/Ring Gauge 44

ROYAL DOMINICANA

Ctry of Manu	Dominican Republic
Filler	Dominican Republic
Binder	Mexico
Wrapper	Connecticut
Flavor	Mild to medium
Quality	Average
Comment	Straightforward tobacco flavors but lacking balance

Vitolas

Name	Length	Ring Gauge
Churchill	7¼in	50
No.1	6¾in	43
Corona	6in	46
Super Fino	6in	35
Nacional	5½in	43
Mini 5's	4in	36

Nacional/5½in/Ring Gauge 43

ROYAL JAMAICA

CTRY OF MANU	DOMINICAN REPUBLIC
FILLER	JAMAICA/DOMINICAN REPUBLIC
BINDER	CAMEROON
WRAPPER	JAVA
FLAVOR	MEDIUM
QUALITY	EXCELLENT
COMMENT	WELL-MADE, WITH THICK AND EARTHY FLAVORS FROM THE START

VITOLAS

NAME	LENGTH	RING GAUGE
No.10 Downing Street	10in	51
Goliath	9in	64
Individuals	8½in	52
Churchill	8in	51
Giant Corona	7½in	49
Double Corona	7in	45
Doubloon	7in	30
Navarro	6¾in	34
Corona Grande	6½in	42
No.2 Tube	6½in	34
Rapier	6½in	28
Park Lane	6in	47
No.1 Tube	6in	45
Director No.1	6in	45
New York Plaza	6in	40
Royal Corona	6in	30
Corona	5½in	40
Buccaneer	5½in	30
Gaucho	5¼in	33
Petit Corona	5in	40
Robusto	4½in	49
Pirate	4½in	30

ROYAL JAMAICA CIGARS

DOUBLE CORONA/7IN/RING GAUGE 45

SAINT LUIS REY

CTRY OF MANU	CUBA
FILLER	CUBA
BINDER	CUBA
WRAPPER	CUBA
FLAVOR	MEDIUM TO FULL
QUALITY	EXCELLENT
COMMENT	PLEASANT TOBACCO FLAVORS WITH A CEDAR AFTERTASTE AND A RICH BUT SLIGHTLY HARSH FINISH

VITOLAS

NAME	LENGTH	RING GAUGE
Churchill	7in	47
Lonsdale	6½in	42
Serie A	5⅝in	46
Corona	5⅝in	42
Regios	5in	48
Petit Corona	5in	42

REGIOS/5IN/RING GAUGE 48

SAINT LUIS REY CIGARS

SANCHO PANZA

CTRY OF MANU	CUBA
FILLER	CUBA
BINDER	CUBA
WRAPPER	CUBA
FLAVOR	MILD
QUALITY	OUTSTANDING
COMMENT	A DELICATE AND SUBTLE SMOKE WITH SUGGESTIONS OF AROMATIC WOODS MINGLED INTO ITS TOBACCO FLAVORS

VITOLAS

NAME	LENGTH	RING GAUGE
Sanchos	$9\frac{1}{4}$in	47
Corona Gigante	7in	47
Molino	$6\frac{1}{2}$in	42
Panetela Largo	$6\frac{1}{2}$in	28
Corona	$5\frac{5}{8}$in	42
Belicosos	$5\frac{1}{2}$in	52
Non Plus	$5\frac{1}{16}$in	42
Bachilleres	$4\frac{5}{8}$in	40

NON PLUS/$5\frac{1}{16}$IN/RING GAUGE 42

SANCHO PANZA CIGARS

SANTA CLARA

CTRY OF MANU	MEXICO
FILLER	MEXICO
BINDER	MEXICO
WRAPPER	MEXICO
FLAVOR	MILD
QUALITY	POOR
COMMENT	A BUCOLIC CIGAR WITH A PREDOMINANT TASTE OF HAY

VITOLAS

NAME	LENGTH	RING GAUGE
No.I	$7\frac{1}{2}$in	52
Premier Tubes	$6\frac{3}{4}$in	38
No.III	$6\frac{5}{8}$in	43
No.II	$6\frac{1}{2}$in	48
No.VI	6in	51
No.V	6in	44
No.VII	$5\frac{1}{2}$in	25
No.IV	5in	44
Robusto	$4\frac{1}{2}$in	50
Quino	$4\frac{1}{4}$in	30

NO.IV/5IN/RING GAUGE 44

SANTA CLARA CIGARS

SANTA DAMIANA

CTRY OF MANU	DOMINICAN REPUBLIC
FILLER	MEXICO/DOMINICAN REPUBLIC
BINDER	DOMINICAN REPUBLIC
WRAPPER	CONNECTICUT
FLAVOR	MILD TO MEDIUM
QUALITY	OUTSTANDIING
COMMENT	VERY WELL MADE WITH GOOD BALANCE AND A CREAMY CHARACTER

VITOLAS

NAME	LENGTH	RING GAUGE
Seleccion No.800	7in	50
Seleccion No.100	6¾in	48
Seleccion No.700	6½in	42
Seleccion No.300	5½in	46
Seleccion No.500	5in	50

NO.300/5½IN/RING GAUGE 46

SOSA

CTRY OF MANU	DOMINICAN REPUBLIC
FILLER	DOMINICAN REPUBLIC/BRAZIL
BINDER	HONDURAS
WRAPPER	ECUADOR
FLAVOR	MEDIUM TO FULL
QUALITY	AVERAGE
COMMENT	A CIGAR OF DISTINCTIVE TOBACCO FLAVORS

VITOLAS

NAME	LENGTH	RING GAUGE
Magnum	7½in	52
Piramides No.2	7in	64
Churchill	7in	48
Lonsdale	6½in	43
Governor	6in	50
Brevas	5½in	43
Wavell	4¾in	50

CHURCHILL/7IN/RING GAUGE 48

SUAVE

CTRY OF MANU	DOMINICAN REPUBLIC
FILLER	DOMINICAN REPUBLIC
BINDER	DOMINICAN REPUBLIC
WRAPPER	CONNECTICUT
FLAVOR	MEDIUM
QUALITY	POOR
COMMENT	LACKING HARMONY AND TASTING OF IMMATURE TOBACCO

VITOLAS

NAME	LENGTH	RING GAUGE
Churchill	7½in	50
Corona	6in	44
Robusto	5in	50

ROBUSTO/5IN/RING GAUGE 50

SUERDIECK

CTRY OF MANU	BRAZIL
FILLER	BRAZIL
BINDER	BRAZIL
WRAPPER	BRAZIL
FLAVOR	MILD TO MEDIUM
QUALITY	AVERAGE
COMMENT	A STINGY DRAW OBSTRUCTED THE FLAVOR, WHICH NEVERTHELESS WAS OF A CURIOUS BUT ACCEPTABLE TOBACCO CHARACTER

VITOLAS

NAME	LENGTH	RING GAUGE
Fiesta	6in	30
Valencia	6in	30
Cabellero	6in	30
Brasilia	5¼in	30
Mandarin Pai	5in	38

VALENCIA/6IN/RING GAUGE 30

SUERDIECK CIGARS

TE-AMO

CTRY OF MANU	MEXICO
FILLER	MEXICO
BINDER	MEXICO
WRAPPER	MEXICO
FLAVOR	MEDIUM
QUALITY	EXCELLENT
COMMENT	SMOOTH, WITH AN UNMISTAKABLE SWEET CHORD

VITOLAS

NAME	LENGTH	RING GAUGE
C.E.O.	8½in	52
Churchill	7½in	50
Maximo	7in	54
Presidente	7in	50
Cabellero	7in	35
Picador	7in	27
Relaxation	6⅝in	44
Torero	$6\frac{9}{16}$in	35
Toro	6in	50
Satisfaction	6in	46
Meditation	6in	42
Elegante	5¾in	27
No.4	5in	42
Impulse	5in	32
Epicure	5in	27
Torito	4¾in	50
Intermezzo	4in	28

TE-AMO CIGARS

RELAXATION/6⅝IN/RIING GAUGE 44

TEMPLE HALL

CTRY OF MANU	JAMAICA
FILLER	MEXICO/JAMAICA/DOMINICAN REPUBLIC
BINDER	MEXICO
WRAPPER	CONNECTICUT
FLAVOR	MILD TO MEDIUM
QUALITY	EXCELLENT
COMMENT	VERY WELL CONSTRUCTED AND WITH A GENEROUS DRAW PROVIDING A GENTLE BALANCE OF SUBTLE TOBACCO FLAVORS

VITOLAS

NAME	LENGTH	RING GAUGE
700	7in	49
685	6⅞in	34
675	6¾in	45
625	6¼in	42
550	5½in	50
500	5in	31
450	4½in	49

450/4½IN/RING GAUGE 49

550/5½IN/RING GAUGE 50

700/7IN/RING GAUGE 49

TEMPLE HALL CIGARS

THOMAS HINDS

CTRY OF MANU	NICARAGUA
FILLER	NICARAGUA
BINDER	NICARAGUA
WRAPPER	NICARAGUA
FLAVOR	MEDIUM
QUALITY	EXCELLENT
COMMENT	RICH TOBACCO WITH FLAVORS OF COFFEE AND NUTS

VITOLAS

NAME	LENGTH	RING GAUGE
Churchill	7in	49
Lonsdale Extra	7in	43
Torpedo	6in	52
Short Churchill	6in	50
Corona	5½in	42
Robusto	5in	50

CHURCHILL/7IN/RING GAUGE 49

VINTAGE HONDURAN

CTRY OF MANU	HONDURAS
FILLER	HONDURAS
BINDER	HONDURAS
WRAPPER	HONDURAS
FLAVOR	MEDIUM
QUALITY	POOR
COMMENT	WATERY IN FLAVOR AND LACKING BALANCE

VITOLAS

NAME	LENGTH	RING GAUGE
Sultans	8½in	52
Imperial	8in	44
President	7½in	50
Panetela Larga	7in	36
Cetro	6½in	44
Governor	6in	50
Panetela	6in	36
Toro	5½in	46
Matador	5½in	42
Rothchild	4½in	50

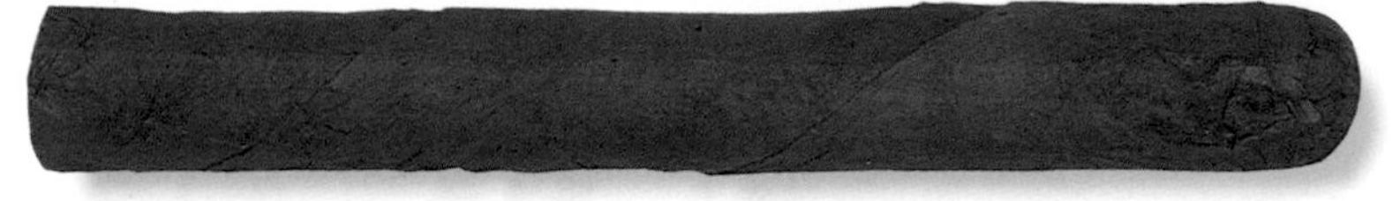

TORO/5½IN/RING GAUGE 46

VUELTABAJO

CTRY OF MANU	DOMINICAN REPUBLIC
FILLER	DOMINICAN REPUBLIC
BINDER	DOMINICAN REPUBLIC
WRAPPER	CONNECTICUT
FLAVOR	MILD TO MEDIUM
QUALITY	AVERAGE
COMMENT	PLEASANT TOBACCO FLAVORS TOGETHER WITH A SUGGESTION OF COCOA WERE APPRECIATED, BUT THE POTENTIAL OF THE BLEND WAS UNDERMINED BY THE CIGAR BEING UNDER-FILLED

VITOLAS

NAME	LENGTH	RING GAUGE
Gigante	8½	52
Churchill	7in	48
Londsdale	7in	43
Toros	6in	50
Corona	5¾in	42
Robusto	4¾in	52

CHURCHILL/7IN/RING GAUGE 48

ZINO

CTRY OF MANU	HONDURAS
FILLER	HONDURAS
BINDER	HONDURAS
WRAPPER	ECUADOR
FLAVOR	MEDIUM TO FULL
QUALITY	AVERAGE
COMMENT	A GOOD BURN AND DRAW BUT WITH RATHER GRITTY TOBACCO FLAVORS

VITOLAS

NAME	LENGTH	RING GAUGE
Mouton Cadet No.1	6½in	44
Mouton Cadet No.2	6in	35
Mouton Cadet No.3	5¾in	36
Mouton Cadet No.4	5⅛in	30
Mouton Cadet No.6	5in	50
Mouton Cadet No.5	5in	44

MOUTON CADET NO.6/5IN/RING GAUGE 50

PART III

RESOURCE GUIDE

PREMIUM CIGAR RING GAUGE GUIDE

RING GAUGE GUIDE

The ring gauge guide gives you a range of commonly found cigar girths. If you wish to check the ring gauge of a cigar you should place it foot first on the different circles until you find a match.

HEAVY RING GAUGE	ALL CIGARS WITH A RING GAUGE OF 45 AND UP.
STANDARD RING GAUGE	ALL CIGARS WITH A RING GAUGE OF 40 TO 44 INCLUSIVE.
SLENDER RING GAUGE	ALL CIGARS WITH A RING GAUGE OF 39 AND UNDER.

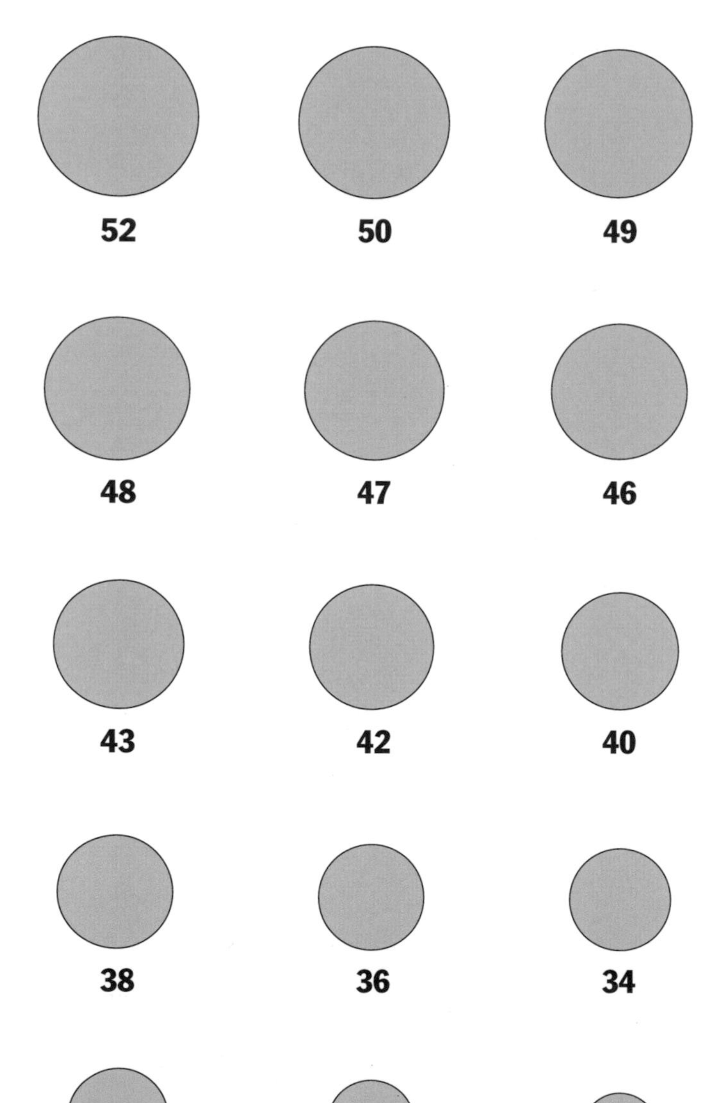

Please remember that the ring gauge of a cigar often shrinks slightly in the *escaparate* and ageing period thereafter. When a cigar is made to a ring gauge of 42 this refers to its diameter just after it leaves the maker's bench.

A cigar's shape may alter either in its packaging, particularly if it is "pressed" to a square shape, or according to the amount of moisture in it.

The numbers represent the diameter of the holes in 64th of an inch, i.e. 48 = $\frac{48}{64}$th or $\frac{3}{4}$ of an inch.

FLAVOR AND QUALITY

The following table shows how the cigars in the directory section of this book are categorized as to flavor and quality, according to the tasting notes and comments of the author.

	POOR	AVERAGE	GOOD	EXCELLENT	OUTSTANDING
MILD	Credo Juan Clemente Santa Clara	Andujar Bering Carlos Torano	C.A.O. Caballeros Dunhill (CI) Juan Lopez Las Cabrillas Leon Jimenes Montesino Nat Sherman Oscar Romeo Y Julieta (DR)	Astral Casa Blanca Dunhill (DR) J.R. Special Jamaican Licenciados Petrus	H. Upmann (C) Macanudo Rafael Gonzalez Sancho Panza
MILD TO MEDIUM	Jose Benito	C.A.O. Gold Jose Marti Royal Dominicana Suerdieck Vueltabajo	Fonseca (DR) Henry Clay La Corona La Diva La Finca Padron Peterson Pleiades	Ashton Avo XO Cuesta-Rey Don Diego El Rey del Mundo (C) Excelsior Habanica H Upmann (DR) Joya de Nicaragua Montecruz Punch (H) Temple Hall	Davidoff Habana Gold Romeo Y Julieta (C) Santa Damiana
MEDIUM	Suave Vintage Honduran	Calixto Lopez La Unica	Bances Belinda Canario D'Oro Don Tomas Felipe Gregorio Gispert J.R. Ultimate Leon Jimenes Matacan Paul Garmirian Por Larranaga (DR)	Bauza Padron Aniversario Primo del Rey Riata Royal Jamaica Te-Amo Thomas Hinds	Arturo Fuente Punch (C)
MEDIUM TO FULL		Bahia Mocha Sosa Zino	Avo Cruz Real Fonseca (C) La Invicta Por Larranaga (C)	Aliados Carlin V. Centennial Diplomaticos Don Lino Don Pepe Hoyo de Monterrey (H) La Gloria Cubana Partagas (DR) Ramon Allones (DR) Saint Luis Rey	Cohiba Cuaba Hoyo de Monterrey (C)
FULL		Baccarat		Bolivar Don Ramos El Rey del Mundo (H) Excalibur	Partagas (C) Ramon Allones (C)

MAJOR CIGAR MANUFACTURERS

This table shows the major cigar manufacturers from the directory section, together with the cigars they produce, and the countries they produce in.

MANUFACTURER	COUNTRY	CIGARS
Agro Tobaco Nicaragua	Nicaragua	Habanica
Briones Montoto	Cuba	Cuaba, Gispert, Romeo Y Julieta, Saint Luis Rey, Sancho Panza
CITA Tabacos de Canarias SA	Canary Isles	Dunhill
Consolidated Cigar Corporation	Honduras, Mexico, Dominican Republic	Don Diego, Dunhill, Henry Clay, H. Upmann, La Corona, Las Cabrillas, Montecruz, Por Larranaga, Primo del Rey, Royal Jamaica, Santa Damiana, Te-Amo
Cuervo Y Hermano	Dominican Republic	Carlos Torano, Peterson
El Laguito	Cuba	Cohiba
Fernando Roig	Cuba	Hoyo de Monterrey, Juan Lopez, Por Larranaga, Punch
Flor de Copan SA	Honduras	Petrus, Zino
Flor de Honduras Tobacco SA	Honduras	Habana Gold
Francisco Perez German	Cuba	Bolivar, La Gloria Cubana, Partagas, Ramon Allones
General Cigar Co.	Jamaica, Dominican Republic	Canario D'Oro, Macanudo, Nat Sherman, Partagas, Ramon Allones, Temple Hall
Heroes del Moncada	Cuba	El Rey del Mundo, Rafael Gonzalez
Inter American Cigars	Honduras	Mocha, Vintage Honduran
La Aurora SA	Dominican Republic	La Aurora, Leon Jimenes
La Real Fabrica du Puros	Honduras	Felipe Gregorio
Jose Marti	Dominican Republic	Diplomaticos, H. Upmann, Montecristo
Matasa	Dominican Republic	Casa Blanca, Fonseca, J.R. Special Jamaican, Licenciados, Romeo Y Julieta, Royal Dominicana
Nestor Plasencia	Nicaragua, Honduras	Bering, Carlin, V Centennial, La Finca
Nueva Matacapan Tabacos SA	Mexico	Excelsior
Padron Cigars	Nicaragua, Honduras	Padron, Padron Aniversario
Puros de Villa Gonzalez	Dominican Republic	La Diva, Suave
Puros Indios Cigars, Inc.	Honduras	Aliados
Ramon Carbonell	Dominican Republic	Jose Marti
Segovia Cigars SA	Nicaragua	C.A.O. Gold
Suerdieck Charutos E Cigharrilhas Ltda.	Brazil	Don Pepe, Suerdieck
Tabacalera A. Fuente Y Cia	Dominican Republic	Arturo Fuente, Ashton, Bauza, Cuesta-Rey, Montesino, Sosa
Tabacalera Santiaguense	Dominican Republic	Juan Clemente
Tabacalera Tambor	Costa Rica	Bahia
Tabacos Puros de Nicaragua	Nicaragua	Joya de Nicaragua, Thomas Hinds
Tabacos Y Puros de San Andres	Mexico	Cruz Real
Tabadom	Dominican Republic	Avo, Avo XO, Davidoff, Griffin's Paul Garmirian
Tampa Rico Cigar Co.	Dominican Republic	Rolando
U.S. Tobacco Co.	Honduras	Astral, Don Tomas
Villazon & Co.	Honduras	Bances, Don Ramos, El Rey del Mundo, Excalibur, Hoyo de Monterrey, J.R. Ultimate, La Invicta, Punch

CIGAR RETAILERS

AUSTRALIA
Benjamin's Fine Tobacco
Melbourne
Tel: (3) 96 63 28 79

Alfred Dunhill
Sydney
Tel: (2) 92 35 16 00

CANADA
Cavendish-Moore's Tobacco Ltd
Calgary
Tel: (403) 269 2716

Havana House
Toronto
Tel: (416) 406 6644
Fax: (416) 406 3340

Old Morris Tobacconist
Victoria
Tel: (250) 382 4811

R.J. Clarke Tobacconist
Vancouver
Tel: (604) 687 4316

Thomas Hinds Tobacconist
Toronto
Tel: (416) 927 9070

FRANCE
A Casa del Habano
Paris
Tel: (331) 45 49 24 30

La Civette
Paris
Tel: (331) 42 96 04 99

GERMANY
Horst Kiwus
Berlin
Tel: (30) 312 4450

Pfeifenhaus Heinrichs
Cologne
Tel: (221) 256 483

Pfeifen Timm
Hamburg
Tel: (40) 345 187

HONG KONG
Cohiba Cigar Divan
Mandarin Oriental Hotel
Tel: (852) 2522 0111
Ext: 4074

Pacific Cigar Company Limited
Wanchai
Tel: (852) 2528 3966
Fax: (852) 2520 6528

SPAIN
Gimeno
Barcelona
Tel: (3) 302 09 83
Fax: (3) 318 49 47

SWITZERLAND
Davidoff & Cie
Geneva
Tel: (41) 223 10 90 41

UNITED KINGDOM
Alfred Dunhill
London, England
Tel: (171) 499 9566
Fax: (171) 499 6471

Davidoff of London
London, England
Tel: (171) 930 3079
Fax: (171) 930 5887

J.J. Fox of St. James
London, England
Tel: (171) 930 3787
Fax: (171) 495 0097

Harrods
London, England
Tel: (171) 730 1234

John Hollingsworth & Son
Birmingham, England
Tel: (121) 236 7768
Fax: (121) 236 3696

Herbert Love
Edinburgh, Scotland
Tel: (131) 225 8082

Saulter of Mayfair
London, England
Tel: (171) 499 4866
Fax: (171) 499 4866

Selfridges
London, England
Tel: (171) 629 1234

The Tobacco House
Glasgow, Scotland
Tel: (141) 226 4586

UNITED STATES
Arnold's Cigar Store
New York, New York
Tel: (212) 697 1477

The Big Easy
Studio City, California
Tel: (812) 762 3279
Fax: (818) 762 2741

Davidoff of Geneva
New York, New York
Tel: (212) 751 9060

Diebels Sportsmens Gallery
Kansas City, Missouri
Tel: (800) 305 2988

Georgetown Tobacco
Washington DC
Tel: (202) 338 5100

Hill Country Humidor
San Marcos, Texas
Tel: (512) 396 7473

Holt Cigar Co.
Philadelphia, Pennsylvania
Tel: (800) 669 1527

Jack Schwartz Importers
Chicago, Illinois
Tel: (312) 782 7898

JR Tobacco
Fairfield, New Jersey
Tel: (201) 882 6446
Fax: (201) 884 1698

JR Tobacco
Statesville, North Carolina
Tel: (704) 872 5300
Fax: (704) 872 8333

Key West Havana Cigar Co.
Key West, Florida
Tel: (305) 296 2680
Fax: (305) 296 2608

Mom's Cigar Shop
New York, New York
Tel: (212) 243 7443
Fax: (212) 243 2034

Nat Sherman
New York, New York
Tel: (212) 246 5500
Fax: (212) 246 8639

The Red Lion Smoke Shop
Salem, Massachusetts
Tel: (508) 745 2050
Fax: (508) 744 7595

Smoke Shop
Hoboken, New Jersey
Tel: (201) 217 1701
Fax: (201) 217 9183

Thompson Cigars
Tampa, Florida
Tel: (813) 804 6344
Fax: (813) 882 4605

ACKNOWLEDGMENTS

The Publisher would like to thank all manufacturers and retailers who made contributions to this book, including Mr Michael D Allen of The Red Lion Smoke Shop (listed), who supplied cigars that proved otherwise unobtainable.

We would also like to thank the following for providing photographs. (While every effort has been made to identify the copyright holders, the Publisher apologises for any omissions made.)

Hold Studios International: pp 10(b), 11(t), 16, 17.

James Davis Travel Photography: pp 8, 9, 10(t,c,), 11 (c,b), 12, 15.

INDEX

Italic page numbers refer to picture captions.